LIFETIME
GUARANTEE

LIFETIME GUARANTEE

Making Your Christian Life Work and What to Do When It Doesn't

Bill Gillham, Ed.D.

with Questions for Discussion by
Preston H. Gillham, M.S.

Wolgemuth & Hyatt, Publishers, Inc.
Brentwood, Tennessee

Published by Wolgemuth & Hyatt, Publishers, Inc.
1749 Mallory Lane, Suite 110, Brentwood, Tennessee 37027.

Printed in the United States of America.

97 96 95 94 93 92 91   8 7

Library of Congress Cataloging-in-Publication Data

Gillham, Bill.
    Lifetime guarantee.

    Bibliography: p. 225.
    1. Christian life—1960-   .   I. Gillham,
    Preston H.   II. Title.

BV4501.2.G51124   1987   248.4   88-17373
ISBN 0-943497-03-5
ISBN 0-943497-39-6 (pbk.)

To my beloved wife Anabel

CONTENTS

ACKNOWLEDGEMENTS

I gratefully acknowledge the Holy Spirit Who worked through the Word and members of the body to teach me the truths contained in this book.

INTRODUCTION

This book is written to the Christian who is struggling in his attempt to live the life of victory in Jesus. It is not a mere glimmer of light at the end of a dark tunnel. Rather, I trust you will discover, as I have, that these truths open wide the door to "the life [that] is hidden with Christ in God" (Col. 3:3).

People usually buy a book on marriage if they've got a problem in their marriage, or they order a book on self-esteem if they've got a low one. But the problem they're actually experiencing is the basic question of how to make the Christian life work. We all have the same problem when you get right down to it.

As I've interacted with thousands of people over my years as a Christian counselor, the hurting person would typically tell me about what counselors refer to as "the presenting problem." I got to where I would sit there with a sort of "hidden agenda," knowing what the *real* problem was but, of course, listening intently and empathetically anyway. I began to see that what they were seeing as their problem was in reality but a symptom of the problem. They were looking for a way to eliminate the symptom, which in their view would solve the problem.

That simply won't work. We all agree that a person with a physical illness who concentrates on eliminating symptoms will have a similar experience to that of the person trying to hold a couple of dozen table tennis balls under water. Think of how absurd it would be to treat your child's fever, which is a symptom of the presence of infection, by packing him in ice! That would lower his temperature, all right, but it would lower the kid, too, by six feet! The fever is not the problem; it is merely a symptom of the underlying trouble.

1

Doctors are trained to treat problems, not symptoms. The symptoms indicate to them the nature of the problem. Once this has been determined, they attack the problem, the *source* of the symptom. Once you correct the problem, many of the symptoms will improve or even disappear.

I've forgotten who said it, but I once heard a preacher say something like this: "Your problem is that you don't know what your problem is. You think your problem is your problem, but that's not the problem at all. Your problem is not your problem, and that's your main problem."

What *is* the problem? Are you ready for this? Here it is. The problem is that you have yet to discover that the Christian life is not difficult to live—it's impossible to live! There it is. In a nutshell. God never intended that you be able to live the Christian life at all. The harder you try to live your life for God, the more frustrated you'll become. But hold the phone! That is precisely the position of weakness and desperation from which the Holy Spirit wants to teach you the reason Jesus came *into* you. Have you ever questioned why He didn't come under you, over you, behind you, or along side you, or in front of you? Jesus is the only one who ever *has* lived the Christian life, and He's the only one who *can* live it today—through you! That's why God can offer a lifetime guarantee of abundant living—and why most believers have yet to experience it.

It's no easier for an ordinary person to live the Christian life today than it ever was. That's the reason you're equipped differently from the average, run-of-the-mill individual. Christ now *indwells* you, Christian, to enable you to cooperate with Him to express *His* life through you moment by moment, not just when you encounter the situations you can't handle by yourself. That's the mistake I made. I tried to handle all the "small stuff" by myself and not trouble Him with it. The straw kept piling up on my back day by day until it inundated me. It took me so long to wake up and smell the coffee! But I think I'm not much different from most people. We're all slow to learn.

What are your symptoms? Troubles in your marriage? You just can't hack it anymore? You're just worn out from trying? You've given and given until you feel as if you just can't give anything else? You're considering bailing out?

Maybe you just can't handle the problems on the job. You're trying to keep all the balls in the air, but you don't have enough hands or time, and they're falling all around your head and shoulders. Your boss doesn't seem to be sympathetic, either. Further, you can't quit because you couldn't get a better job. And, once you found out that *Maranatha* means "Come quickly, Lord," you've been closing your prayers with it ever since.

Perhaps you go off to the convention and you wind up in the massage parlor or renting a porno movie in your hotel room — or something worse. You've promised God you'll never do it again, but you have. You've rededicated until your rededicator's worn out, and nothing helps. And you're a teacher, or a deacon — or a pastor?

Maybe your attitude about yourself is "If I could just become a different person! Someone I could learn to like and respect! But [sigh] what's the use? It's all so hopeless! I've tried the self-improvement books and tapes. They just don't work for me. I'm just different. I'd be better off dead. Everyone would be better off if I were gone! I can't stand myself!" And maybe you've even toyed with the notion of ending it all.

Dear one, it is no accident that you've picked up this book. This is your time! Our precious Lord wants to offer some beautiful, healing words to you from these pages. All that garbage listed above is one deep pile of (you guessed it) *symptoms*. Your problem is two-fold:

Number 1, you are trying to live the Christian life instead of understanding how to collaborate with Christ to live the Christian life *for* you and *through* you. *Number 2*, you are not comprehending how to appropriate your true identity as the new creation you already are *in* Christ. You are still attempting to face each day using your old I.D. pass.

I hear you say, "But I don't understand that." I didn't, either, when I was in my fix. But, I'm free from my fix now. He took me through it, and I'm here to tell you it was a big one. God spells relief *J-e-s-u-s*. Wouldn't you know that appropriating some facet of Christ is somehow the root of the solution for every problem that any person can experience? The key to experiencing victory in Christ lies in learning how to literally "walk in newness of life" as described in the Word.

God has graciously shown me how to appropriate the life that is hidden with Christ and to explain it in very simple, Biblical terms. I guess my strong suit is simple communication through practical life experiences, the nuts and bolts kind, to teach you how to see Christ glorify Himself through *you*.

Let me draw you a verbal road map to acquaint you with this book. It is designed to teach you *how* to appropriate consistent, rather than just sporadic, victory in Christ.

In Chapter 1, we'll look at how you have programmed your brain with earthly techniques for satisfying your needs for love and self-esteem—the greatest needs in life—rather than seeking these through Christ. These *techniques* are called "flesh" by God (see Phil. 3:3-6).

In Chapter 2, we'll see that the measure of success or failure you attain in satisfying your needs through earthly techniques determines your unique version of the flesh. Those who are successful cling to these; those who are not feel hopelessly unlovely. *Both* are flesh. In Chapter 3, I describe my own struggle for love and self-esteem to help you identify your flesh.

In Chapters 4 and 5, we'll deal with the fact that you were born a self-centered rebel, dead to God, but alive to Satan and the world. Your major goal was to get all your needs supplied *your* way. God had no plan to make something beautiful of *your* self-centered life, but to crucify it in Christ and spawn a *new* creature in Him who is now totally acceptable *to* Him.

In Chapter 6, we'll examine how Satan tries to deceive you. His goal is to trick you into using your flesh to get your God-given needs satisfied. He accomplishes this goal through your thought life, masquerading as the now defunct "old man."

In Chapter 7, we'll emphasize the reality of who you are as a Christian. When you were born, your parents didn't say, "Oh, I hope he matures into a human being." *Birth* determined your identity. You *are* human. Likewise, when God caused you to be born brand new in Christ, He didn't say, "Oh, I hope he turns out to be a new creature in Christ." Your *second* birth determines your *present* spiritual identity.

In Chapter 8, we'll consider the role of feelings. Feelings are wonderful when they line up with *God's* reality. The problem is that they also react to earthly circumstances. This is when you are most highly motivated to "walk after the flesh" rather than to walk in the finished work of Christ *for* you *in* the circumstance.

In Chapter 9, we'll see how Christ living through you is supposed to be the typical Christian experience. Many believers are deceived into thinking that trusting Christ as your life is an idealistic fantasy for them, something attained only by a spiritual elite. Quite the contrary is true. Such a life isn't only attainable; it is God's provision for *every* Christian.

In Chapter 10, we'll examine Bible verses that seem to refute this teaching. The Bible can be interpreted as teaching that salvation, security, and sanctification must be earned. But it can also be interpreted that these are *bestowed* upon the believer solely by grace through faith in the finished work of Christ. The correct interpretation is critical to your victory over the flesh. This chapter reveals what I believe is the key to "rightly dividing the word of truth" (2 Tim. 2:15).

In Chapter 11, we'll discuss the need for "brokenness." Most of us have only a hazy understanding of what we're to be broken *from*. We must be broken from trusting in our fleshly ways. Often they have been so productive that God must allow suffering that our flesh can't handle to come into our lives.

Finally, in Chapter 12, we'll see that God's ultimate goal is to conform you to Christ's image, and we'll review how He does that. Snuffing Satan out will be easy for God when the time comes. But right now, God is using him by allowing him to attack your flesh. God's goal is that you be motivated to abandon your fleshly ways and turn to Him, learning to enjoy His lifetime guarantee.

I'm not a trained theologian, although that would be nice. I'm just pretty much a plain vanilla guy who mows the lawn, marvels at how airplanes fly, feels he's gathering precious treasure when his pecan tree bears in the fall, watches football games, loves his wife and kids, and loves Jesus with all his heart.

God has freed me from a life of hostility and criticism toward my wife and sons; from lusting after anything in a skirt; from demanding that my sons be macho; from being torn by passions within, doubting my self-worth and at times my salvation, and yet simultaneously working like crazy trying to live a life of victory in Christ. After twelve years of struggling, I finally crashed and burned.

That was the best thing the Lord could have ever let happen to me. It was through my painful failure after giving the Christian life my best shot that God began to teach me the liberating truths recorded in this book. I know of no other book quite like it. If I did, I wouldn't have undertaken this project. I do not intend to toot my own whistle or claim to have the market cornered on truth. God has dealt with that. "I will not presume to speak of anything except what Christ has accomplished *through me*" (Rom. 15:18, emphasis added). This book and the freedom I now enjoy through the truths it contains, I respectfully dedicate to my hero, Jesus.

I am also indebted to my son and partner in the ministry, Pres, for his technical expertise and wisdom in writing this book. He has also developed study questions following each chapter. If you want the contents of this book to become more than simply information, I urge you to work through these study helps as an aid to personal appropriation.

I love you,
Bill Gillham, Ed.D.

O N E

WHY YOU STRUGGLE

The following suicide note came to me in January 1986:

> I can't stand living anymore. For an eternity, it seems, I have done little but exist. I am of no use to anyone, especially God. There is so much in my head that I know He wants me to do for myself, but I just seem incapable of willing myself to do anything—especially about my mental state. Suicide seems to be the only solution left.
>
> I'm sure people will not understand. They will think that it was senseless to waste such a young life. That is exactly how I feel: it *is* senseless. But, since I *am* wasting my life anyway, I might as well do something! I will do the only thing I believe I can do—stop existing.
>
> There is no way to explain this to people. No one can understand the torment a person goes through day after day unless they themselves have been mentally ill. No matter how much people say they love me and no matter how much they encourage me to pull myself out of this, it still doesn't help; I simply don't know how to help myself. I've tried other people's suggestions—including committing yourself to a psych ward—and nothing helps. Over and over again the message is the same: "You have to help yourself." But no one can tell me *how* to help myself.
>
> Do you see why suicide is my only alternative? What would you do? Where would you go if you didn't know how to help yourself? What would you do to stop feeling so helpless, to stop feeling like such a failure for not being the Christian you know Christ wants you to be? What would you do?
>
> What would you do if year after miserable year you only seemed to take up space—space no one seemed to care about or notice anyway. I could commit suicide and literally not be discovered for weeks, maybe even months!

Christ said that I am to be the salt of the earth. I can hardly stand to do the bare minimum each day to exist, let alone care for anyone else. There was a time in my life when this was so different. A time when I exhausted myself with labor for others. But as time went by, I began to see that Christ wasn't enough in my life. I needed and wanted something more. I tried to keep working toward the goal of helping others, but I just got more and more drained until now I am mentally ill.

Christ said that I was to be the light of the world. My light has been reduced to a flicker. In fact, it is worse than flickering; it is now smoking from having just been blown out.

What a waste. Is there any hope? Christians would say, "Yes." They would point to a relationship with Christ, and I would agree if I could only see it again. If I could only feel it again.

What would you say to this young woman? Would you say she needs professional help? Some years ago that's what I would have said—before I began to comprehend the truths set forth in this book.

Exactly one year later, I met this dear lady at a seminar Anabel, my wife, and I were leading in Washington, D.C. The woman is now a happy, productive, relaxed Christian who praises Christ daily. In the postscript of a more recent letter from her, she said, "Just today I brought a woman into my home the doctors feel should enter the psych ward. Who would have thought a year ago when I was planning my death that God would be using me to help someone who is so desperate?" And she signed off with a smiley face.

The Flesh

The truths contained in this book are precious, fine gold. I can say that without feeling I'm bragging because they aren't mine. I have merely been entrusted with them to pass them on to others. For you to understand them, we must proceed step by step, the first of which is to give you an extended understanding of what the Bible means when it speaks of "flesh" or "walking after the flesh" (see e.g. Rom. 8:4). The suicidal woman's lack of understanding of this concept almost destroyed her.

In these first two chapters, then, I'll show how you have pro-grammed your brain with earthly techniques for satisfying your needs for love and self-esteem — again, the greatest needs in life — *or* for believing yourself to be unworthy of either and thus living your life to keep love away because it makes you uncom-fortable. Both of these techniques are do-it-yourself projects that God calls "flesh." I'll document this later from Philippians 3:3-9.

The term "flesh" has many meanings in the Bible, but our primary definition here is this: *flesh refers to the old ways or patterns by which you have attempted to get all your needs supplied instead of seek-ing Christ first and trusting Him to meet your needs*. These patterns de-velop as you are growing up in your parents' home. And when the Holy Spirit begins the work of tearing them down, most Christians panic at the idea of losing them.

We can lump all Christians into three broad flesh categories: Yukky Flesh, Plain Vanilla Flesh, and USDA Choice Flesh. The person with the Yukky Flesh has been reared in an environment where, no matter how hard he tried, he couldn't get his love sup-ply out of it by his do-it-yourself tactics. The suicidal woman at the beginning of this chapter has Yukky Flesh. She was nearly deceived into suicide to escape her feelings of low self-esteem. The Plain Vanilla, or average, Flesh person has been moderately successful, neither a roaring success nor a total failure at getting his need for self-esteem met. The USDA Choice Flesh person is everyone's candidate for Mr. Christian. His high self-esteem is a result of his skill at milking love out of the world.

We're going to look at how all three flesh types get pro-grammed into Christians. For economy's sake, however, I'll only describe in greater detail the structuring of Yukky Flesh. You can then apply how that happens to the development of the other two.

How Does God Spell "Relief"? (Step 1)

The Word teaches that God *is* love and that He loves us (see 1 John 4:9, 10). God created humanity with a burning need for love. That's why you're sitting there needing love. If you didn't need love, you wouldn't need God. In fact, that's why you were created with needs, period. God is the supreme authority figure who has the market cornered on being able to supply all our needs. Thus, He created a bunch of people who have a ton of needs. This way, some of us would recognize our need and turn to Him through Jesus to get our needs supplied *His* way. God spells relief *J-e-s-u-s*. Fleshly people spell it *s-e-l-f* ("I'll do it *my* way").

The Problem: Lord of the Ring (Step 2)

When you showed up on planet earth in a little earthsuit two feet long, you drew a circle around yourself and declared, "I am Lord of this Ring!" Oh, you were willing to let God run the universe, but your attitude was "*I* am god of all the turf inside this circle. I will control *this* area." Playing Lord of the Ring is what original sin is all about. Adam saw to it that you'd be a "born" loser, and you immediately began to demonstrate it. You knew nothing about God and His provision for supplying all your needs, so you took over His role. Since most of your other needs were being met pretty well, you looked to Mom, Dad, siblings, relatives, and later to peers to satisfy your need for love. That cut God out of His own picture.

How Little Children Learn
About Themselves (Step 3)

A preschool child is the most self-centered creature God ever made; he thinks only of himself and his needs. This being true, *he learns only of himself* as he interacts with others. When the dad of a nine-month-old baby points to his own nose and then to that of his teensy offspring and says, "Nose," the little one doesn't reason, *How interesting! Dad and I both have noses!* Oh, no. He thinks *I've got a nose and it looks like that.* Total, self-centered thinking.

Who Am I?

Let's consider what a little child learns who is born to a couple who had to get married due to his unexpected arrival. Let's name him Charlie. His mom and dad were only sixteen when they were forced into marriage by both sets of parents. Charlie's imminent arrival caused the newlyweds to drop out of high school in their junior year, which "ruined their lives."

The little daddy had his heart set on being a college athlete and someday a football coach, but Charlie shattered that dream. It's now three years later, and Dad works at the local Dairy Queen for seventy-five dollars a week. The onset of football season is always agony for him as he meditates on lost opportunities and a hopeless future. He broods a lot over the "life sentence" he's serving with no hope of time off for good behavior. Color him hostile.

The little mom had always wanted to be a sorority girl at her mom's alma mater. Mom and her mother before her were both members. In fact, they both still wear their pins at homecoming. This was a "big thing" for her in her childhood, but now, at nineteen, she works at the local Kentucky Fried Chicken restaurant.

Her friends come home from the university on weekends in their fancy new clothes, but she still has to wear her old high school wardrobe, which is now outdated. She listens to their exciting stories of campus life, and she sees their manicured nails, expensive hairdos, polished toenails, and so on—all the result of their being able to invest hours per week on their earthsuits. She is bitter and resentful. She, too, sees herself serving a life sentence for having made one fatal mistake. And to make matters worse, it was *his* idea.

The romantic side of marriage for her has long since dissipated. Sex is more of an obligation than a romantic oasis, "just one more thing I have to do for that louse who ruined my life!" It's sort of like cooking another batch of chicken, only after closing hours! Color her despairing.

There are basically two sorts of folks on planet earth, "ulcer-givers" and "ulcer-getters." These two are ulcer-givers; they give them to other folks, mainly to each other. They keep a hot war going on constantly in their little, three-room house. Right at the height of the battle (words, not fists), Dad will unleash a verbal artillery salvo on Charlie. "It's all *your* fault, you little bleepity bleep! If *you* hadn't come along, I wouldn't be married to this old bat! I wish you'd never been born!" And he storms out of the house in a rage, to the accompanying tune of his wife's screaming that she hopes he'll get lost and never be found.

The Results

Now, moment by moment, day by day, who is Charlie learning about? Is he learning, *Now, wait a minute, Dad! I didn't ask to be born into this chicken outfit?* No, he's learning about himself, remember? He's processing the situation like this: *It's all my fault that Mom and Dad are so miserable and unhappy! If I were gone, it'd be better for everybody! I am the problem! I really do need love, but I don't blame Mom and Dad for not loving me. If I were in their shoes, I wouldn't love me either! Sorry, no-good bum! Anybody that would cause the very ones he loves the most to be miserable ought to be shot! I hate myself!* Obviously, he doesn't verbalize it as I have done, but it's all coming through to him at the gut level.

Charlie's family environment represents the whole world to him because it's the only world he knows. Therefore, he generalizes his attitude to this: *The whole world would be better off if I had never been born.*

The Plot Thickens (Step 4)

You have a mind and you have emotions, a "thinker" and a "feeler." Your feeler responds to your thinker; whatever you set your thinker on, your feeler will react to it. For example, suppose there's a rattlesnake on the floor coiled to strike you on the leg, and you see it poised. First, you will detect this stimulus with your mind, which responds, *I* believe *I'm in great danger!* Let's quantify this on a one to ten scale, where ten is the greatest. *I believe I'm in great danger, and that's a ten!* Now, feeler responds to mind's belief like this: *I feel terrified, and that's a ten!*

Then, suppose that on closer examination you detect that the snake is made of rubber. Mind says, *Why, there's no danger here; I* believe *I'm safe.* And mind immediately goes back down to level one. But what about feeler? Does it go immediately back to one? No way! Oh, it'll eventually go down all right, but it'll take thirty minutes to do so. It'll go down like a B.B. sinking in oil.

Now let's say that your mind's gone down to one, and in ten minutes your feeler is down to about a seven. Then you open a drawer that's got a spider in it, and the spider scoots up your sleeve! Your mind goes from one to ten instantly, and feeler covers the three points back to the top in one leap.

Generalizing from this illustration, let me pose a question. What if you are reared in a home where your dad is a rattlesnake and your mom is a spider? Or maybe it's your brother or an aunt or a surrogate, like Grandma. They keep your mind *and* your feeler at level ten most of the time. When they back off for a few minutes, your mind will go down to one and think, *Whew, relief at last!* But feeler only gets down to about a seven when one of them does it to you again. Wham! Bam! Ten and ten! Due to this process, do you see that by the time you are five years old, it's been so long since your feeler's been below a seven that it sort of bottoms out on seven? *Seven becomes the floor, or threshold, below which your feeler does not go.* This is what happens to a child like Charlie.

Psychologists teach that by the time a child reaches age five, 85 percent of his personality is established and is irreversible. Unfortunately, those psychologists never heard of 2 Corinthians 5:17, which says that any person *in* Christ is a *new* creation, that old things *have* passed away, and that *all* things *are* new. What psychologists are observing is that kids' feelers get programmed, and this controls the person throughout his entire life. But praise God, we walk by *faith*, not by *feel*. There is a way out.

Does Your Elevator Go Clear Down to the Lobby?

Now suppose Charlie grows up and gets saved by accepting Christ as his personal Lord and Savior. God may do many glorious works to erase some of his hangups, but He doesn't erase them all, and I find that in the vast majority of cases the adult who has had childhood experiences such as I have described has his feeler stuck on about a seven or even a 9.5. It's been so long since the points below seven on his emotional Richter Scale have been exercised that they've atrophied away like the arm muscles in a cast. After many years, they aren't even operative any longer. They're like a 1935 Buick that's been sitting in a little old lady's garage since World War II. It has all the standard equipment, but it sure won't run! Its parts are stuck. It needs to be freed up. And the Holy Spirit is the oil who can deal with the problem I'm describing.

The Beat Goes On (Step 5)

God has designed the human brain with memory banks. They're just like the First National Bank, only instead of being a depository for money, they are depositories for memories. Your memory banks have memory traces burned across them. These are habit patterns of how you *act*, how you *feel*, and how you *think*. The more you repeat these patterns, the more deeply entrenched they become. This is the usual method for their development, although a memory trace may become deeply imprinted in just one (often traumatic) episode.

Some of these memory traces are fine such as your particular language pattern. These patterns were etched into your memory banks through your experiences, and your speech is now "controlled" by this. And the Lord doesn't get concerned about whether you sound as if you were reared in California or New York.

Memory traces are like highways, and the more you drive on them, the wider they become. Traffic flow is the key to development and maintenance. The more you spend your time in the pattern, the stronger it becomes. I suppose you're sitting there with several thousand of them ranging from eight-laners to cow trails. Some of them are okay, but some of them are sheer garbage in God's ecology. Let's color these green for garbage. These green highways were generated by the "old man" as he sought to get his needs supplied on planet earth using *his* resources and cutting God out of the picture. He (the old man) was his own god. He declared himself Lord of the Ring.

. . . And On (Step 6)

With that understanding, we can see that little Charlie, having been reared with rejection, *learned* that he was yukky. He was trained like a bird dog to accept as "truth" that he really *is* yukky. And now his feeler is stuck on a threshold of eight, having not been below an eight in years. Digits one through seven are non-existent. They have atrophied away. As he becomes more and more aware of "who he is" (yukky), his feeler will become more and more programmed. This has become a monstrous, green highway for him. He feels yukky most of the time.

The "New Math"

As Charlie matures, he becomes more astute in his observations of the world, better able to objectively assess truth. The only trouble is that since his feeler is stuck on eight and always has been so far as he's able to recall, he now has renumbered his emotional Richter Scale. Since eight is as low as he's ever experienced, he now calls "eight" a "one."

Do you see, then, that Charlie can go from his "one" up to ten five times faster than someone who's playing with a full deck? He's got only two points on his Richter Scale. But he doesn't *know* that. He just knows that he reacts internally (or externally) five times as rapidly as other kids do, and then he "objectively" concludes that he's weird. I use quotation marks around the word *objectively* because Charlie will assure you that he *knows* he's weird. He believes he has arrived at this conclusion objectively, when, in fact, he has arrived at it by virtue of how he feels. This is *his* normal experience. He typically hates himself and wishes he were someone different, someone he could love.

The Noose Tightens (Step 7)

If you identify with this category I've been discussing, don't hear me making light of you. I know it may be painful to have me dredging up all this trauma from your past, but trust me that the Lord has shown me some solid answers.

Now let's grow Charlie up to adulthood. His feeler has been stuck for so long that its programming is as deep as the Grand Canyon. He has built his life around rejection. He rejects himself and others, being unable to trust them. He believes that if he gets too close to them, they will hurt him or discover how yukky he really is and turn away from him. Thus, he has learned that it's safer to just keep everyone away. If anyone earnestly tries to show love to him, even his wife or kids, he will be skeptical of it. Since he hates himself, anyone who tries to love him must be either pretty dumb or else a phony.

What does Charlie do then? He runs tests on the love others offer to see if it will break down. When it does (and it usually will due to techniques he has learned to employ), something inside him seems to "fall into place." *I* knew *it! I* knew *it!* he thinks. *I* knew *she didn't love me! I just had this* feeling. *She fooled me for fourteen years, but her true colors finally showed!* Or if the lover's love does not break down, Charlie may actually drive the lover away, being unable to tolerate the love. He wants it, but he can't handle it. He's like a dog chasing a car and finally catching it: "What do I do with this?" He has never experienced a love environment before and he can't handle it.

At the other extreme, if Charlie ever tastes love, he may latch onto it like white on rice. I've seen more than one Yukky-Flesh mother who smothers her kids, often producing lots of them "because I love kids." She then strives to keep them dependent on her so she can extract *her* love supply out of them, while simultaneously alienating them with her counterproductive methods. Thus she winds up rejected again and "proves" that she really is yukky.

If you try to be kind to such a person at Sunday school, she shows up on your front porch after lunch "just to visit with such a nice person." She leaves at 10:30 P.M., but not before learning how many days you have free this week so she can come over and "enjoy good Christian fellowship." Now she's sucking her love supply out of you. It will begin to drive you up the wall. Then Satan will work the false guilt number on *you* as you begin to resent her taking up so much of your time.

I've also seen some folks with the rejection patterning who are all peaches and cream one day and who will give you the cold shoulder for no reason. They are the vacillators; they jump from one of these polarities to the other without predictability. Once you see what's happening to these dear people, it will become easier for you to discern the cause of these symptoms.

The Finishing Touch (Step 8)

Let's return to Charlie's childhood and use the rattlesnake illustration again to add the finishing touch to his emotions. If little Charlie *believes* in his mind that he is worthless to his parents, how will he *feel?* Worthless! When he matures, his feeler will be stuck, feeling worthless at, say, level nine. If he believes he's inadequate, how will his emotions get programmed? He will feel inadequate (say, at level seven). If he believes he's ugly, he will feel ugly. If he believes he's a loser, he will feel he's a loser. If he believes he's responsible for all the misery in his house (which is his *world*), how will he feel? He'll feel guilty.

Is Charlie guilty? No! He's not guilty of anything. His parents are doing him a great disservice. They are being used by Satan to strap unmerited guilt on their son. That's *false* guilt.

Emotions Lie

Here's a crucial point, so underline it: false guilt *feels* exactly like valid guilt (a conviction from the Holy Spirit). You can't tell the difference by how they *feel*. Your feeler will return the same verdict for both. Guilty! The jury is fixed as far as the feeler is concerned!

Because this is true, you have to look to the Word of God for discernment to determine whether any guilt is valid or false. The Word is the path to truth, not your emotions. Emotions are fine things, but emotions will lie to you at times; the Word of God never will. You've got to know whether you are guilty or not from the Bible. False guilt comes from the Evil One, working through the flesh (old patterns in the brain). Valid guilt comes from the Holy Spirit working through your spirit (see Figure 1.1).

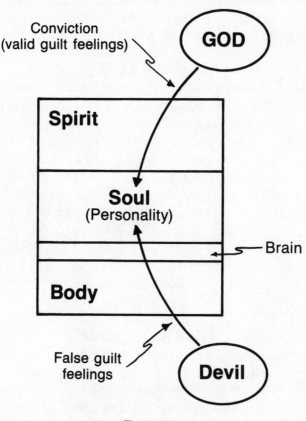

Figure 1.1

You can confess false guilt through the night until sunrise and it'll never get better. In fact, it'll get worse! You will greet the dawn after your night of confession *feeling* guiltier because you still feel guilty. You must never confess false guilt to God as if it were valid. You must agree with God's Word that you are not guilty and deny that the guilt is valid. You don't deny that you *feel* guilty, but you deny that you *are* guilty. You confess, "Praise God! I am not guilty! Even though it *is* true that I have committed sins against the Lord, I have repented and confessed these to You, Sir, and I am forgiven! Praise God I am forgiven! I am not guilty! You said so, Lord! Hallelujah!" (Stage whisper: "Lord, I sure do *feel* guilty, though.")

(Stage whisper back: "Yes, your feeler's stuck, Son, but you keep hanging in there on what *I* said about whether you're guilty or not. I'll begin to unstick it for you as you 'set your mind on things above.' I'll give you more points to play with on your Richter Scale. You're going to grow to where you can tolerate this false guilt number and slough it off with truth.")

Yukky Flesh (Step 9)

Obviously, adult Charlie has a problem. He set out as an infant to get all his needs supplied by himself, doing it his way. But the deck was stacked against him as far as getting love was concerned. There was no way he was going to make it. So, while on this self trip, he gets rejected, is trained to believe he's a loser, and thus learns to reject himself. His feeler gets programmed for non-love, and he develops skills in how to live with rejection. This becomes his "turf." It's where he functions best. He'll gravitate to rejection or generate it, because it's on this turf that he's best able to function. However, since God created him to *need* love, he's miserable! He can't tolerate love or believe it's real if he does get it. His Lord-of-the-Ring approach isn't working for him. He's a very unhappy person.

Plain Vanilla Flesh

Consider now the average person (who may be reading this book). We'll call him Joe. He got a pretty fair share of love as a child. Oh, sure, he may have been rejected off and on by certain people during the course of his life, but all in all, he has experienced a pretty good measure of acceptance. Unbeknownst to him, however, the love he has received has not been received without his having paid for it. People don't usually love you with no strings attached; you must earn their love. A child must perform up to certain standards in order to be "loved." Since he desperately needed love on a moment-by-moment basis, he was willing to pay whatever performance price was demanded in order to receive it. All things considered, he was pretty fair at playing Lord of the Ring. These techniques are very precious to him. He relies heavily on them to generate and maintain love from others and for self.

USDA Choice Flesh

Consider next a home where the dad is a moderately successful businessman, works fairly hard, has built his business by increasing its size, is rather perfectionistic in several areas, and has, on many occasions, philosophized on the merits of such a lifestyle to his son Sam. Dad's system of reward (praise) and punishment has been predicated upon these standards that characterize his life.

Now Dad would probably insist that his acceptance of his young son is *not* based on whether Sam can emulate his dad's performance. But the youngster gets a different message. You see, he is living in a hostile world, peopled by peers who demand that he dance to their tune if they are to "pay him off" with acceptance for services rendered. He begins to take for granted the notion that acceptance is available on this planet, but that it comes with a price tag on it. That price tag is performance. And he's able to pay for it. He has enough talent, intelligence, looks, and whatever else is needed to earn love from people.

What has *he* learned? How has *he* been trained on this planet? Why, he's a winner! He plays Lord of the Ring very well. Oh, sure, he's lost a few in his day, but nothing that has been so devastating that he couldn't cope and ultimately land on his feet. And through it all, he has learned to accept (love) himself. He takes for granted that he can beat Joe. And he can't identify with Charlie at all. He may even feel compassion for Charlie and wonder why he can't get his act together.

Do you see that *all* these men have cut Christ out of their lives as *the* source? They're as lost as a ball in high weeds! It's just that one's god-playing trip is unproductive, whereas the others' god-playing is "working."

Walking After the Flesh

Now, let's have them each accept Jesus Christ as Savior. After salvation, they will each begin to demonstrate different versions of the same problem—walking after the flesh. Let me explain briefly here how this works, but more at length in the ensuing chapters.

Charlie hears all about how much God loves him, but he can't seem to "feel" the way he "feels" other Christians "feel." It would appear on the surface that Joe and Sam are relatively free from this problem, but not so. They *feel* good. They feel loved, and since the techniques they've used all their lives to generate acceptance from others as well as self are still productive, they continue to employ them. Only this time they apply them to the Church environment. They simply tack a few appropriate Scriptures onto their existing good feelings about themselves and "feel" they're now walking in the Spirit.

"My strength is made perfect in weakness," the Lord told the Apostle Paul (2 Cor. 12:9, KJV). I love Ken Taylor's paraphrase in the Living Bible: "My power shows up best in weak people." Since Charlie is weak and knows without a doubt that he's weak, he's a super candidate for God's strength to "show up best in." But how about Joe and Sam? They thank God daily that they're strong! They mean well, but they're flying on flesh power and heading for a flameout.

Here's the point to remember: *Now that these three men are saved, the Evil One will try to control each of them by working through their old patterning.* He'll try to use Charlie's flesh to *block* him from appropriating love and self-esteem through Christ's finished work for him. This was happening to the young woman who wrote the suicide note that began this chapter. The Evil One was seeking to destroy her through her Yukky Flesh. On the other hand, he'll try to deceive both the Plain Vanilla Flesh person and Mr. Wonderful into settling for a cheap imitation of the valid article, trusting in the same old fleshly techniques they have always used to generate acceptance from others and from self. Now re-read this paragraph, please. It's that important.

Conclusion

Perhaps you have been able to identify with one of these types of flesh. If yours is the rejection pattern, you must see that by striving to adjust to the world's demands so you can gain others' acceptance and accept yourself, you are still caught in the flesh trap. If, on the other hand, you identify more with the people who managed to "make it" through techniques found in the "self-help" section of your local library, you are no different from the man who identifies with Charlie. You just *feel* better. Your flesh is paying off with the world's (and, alas, the Church's) acceptance, where his is not. Both positions are sin positions, failing to trust God to supply all your needs in Christ Jesus.

There is no such thing as Spirit-filled flesh, although you see a lot of teachers who are trying to market and package this product. How are you attempting to get your love needs met? *How does your method for getting acceptance differ from that of the lost man or woman?* You programmed these patterns into yourself during your childhood as you sought to get all your needs supplied, primarily your need for love. This constitutes your unique version of the flesh. Do you still depend on it? The precious Holy Spirit wants to reveal to you what Christ has made available to you to liberate you from "walking after the flesh" to get your acceptance needs met in Him. Ask the Lord to reveal this truth to you from His Word as you study this book. We are totally accepted, brother, in Christ! It's not necessarily a feeling; it's a *fact*. It is to be primarily *believed*, not felt.

Questions for Further Study

1. God created you with a need for love. Why is this?

2. The ability to think abstractly begins to develop during the elementary school years. This means that children are basically concrete thinkers, primarily thinking only of themselves. Of what significance is this when trying to determine how your flesh was structured?

3. What kinds of things have you based your self-acceptance on, and through what means have you tried to get acceptance from others?

4. In what specific ways have you tried to play god and get
   your needs met your way?

HOW YOU GOT
INTO YOUR FIX

One night some years ago, I was invited to dinner in the home of a member of the church in which I was speaking. The couple's son, his wife, and their one-year-old flew in from out of state shortly after I arrived. It's always neat to see people warmly greeting each other, but this visit took a sudden nosedive. It seems the baby's diaper bag was missing, and Mama began to let Daddy know in no uncertain terms whose fault it was. The poor guy was calmly trying to reassure her that this was the termination of the flight, that it was probably still on the plane, that he'd call his friend who worked at the airport, and that they could pick it up the next day.

She lit into him like a tiger, however, and *ordered* him back into the car, telling him not to come back without that bag. That's when he, feeling emasculated in front of his own folks and a stranger, retaliated. But brother, he made no headway. She was acting out the role of headship in that relationship, and she made no effort to conceal it.

This young woman is a Christian. Surprised? "How can a new creature in Christ act like Satan himself is controlling her?" you ask. It's easy. We see it every day, don't we? The Bible calls it "walking after the flesh," and she was simply demonstrating her unique version of it for the whole world to see. It brings great dishonor to the name of Christ, but I could identify with her. I've done things even worse than that. As a result of learning the things I discuss in this book, however, I've seen Christ live through me to drastically reduce such episodes to a trickle of what they once were.

Have you ever pondered the question posed by Romans 7:15: "Why do I do what I do, when I really don't want to do it?" I know exactly why. It's because I sometimes walk after the flesh. But for a long time, I didn't know what my flesh is. And how could I know I was free unless I got a handle on just what it was I needed to be free from? You likewise need to gain insight into your unique version of the flesh. That's the purpose of this chapter.

On the surface, you might get the idea as you read along that this chapter deals with child-rearing. But I'm dealing with the structuring of your flesh. Since you began playing Lord of the Ring in infancy, that's where it began getting choreographed, so I must deal with it there.

Caution: make it your major purpose as you read this chapter to learn from the Holy Spirit what happened to *you* as a child, then your secondary purpose to see any mistakes you may be making with your own children. It's primarily *your* flesh we're interested in exposing.

Righteousness

Let's start by coming to a common understanding of the term "righteousness." This understanding alone could revolutionize your life. You can consider the term righteousness from two viewpoints: (1) righteous works (behavior); or (2) righteous identity (state of being).

It's my conviction that most Christians think only of righteous performance — holy behavior — when they think of righteousness. Of course, godly behavior is important. Biblically it refers to "righteous works." But the Word is very clear (see e.g., Gal. 3:6-9 and Rom. 4:9-13) that there is a righteousness *that is absolutely unrelated to performance*. It is a declaration by God of a person's identity. He says that He will declare a person righteous under one condition — if the person is hidden in Christ by faith.

Using this definition of righteous, then, it means that God *declares* a person accepted, "right" with Him. The tragedy is that most people who have been declared "all right" by God continue to strive to generate their own declaration of being "all right." The Bible refers to this as "dead works."

Biblical Definition of Flesh

Next we need a Biblical definition of "flesh." In Philippians 3:3-9, we find a very clear explanation. This passage leaves no doubt that the term "flesh" in this context refers to the Christian's "old ways." Please don't misunderstand me: the term "flesh" does not refer to the Christian's *body* in this context. The body is not the "bad guy." God made the whole man and redeems the whole man — spirit, soul, *and body*. In other Biblical contexts, the term "flesh" is sometimes used to refer to the body, but here the term simply means the Christian's old ways.

I wish to make ten points concerning this passage that will give us a better idea of what it means to "walk after the flesh." (I would encourage you to look this passage up in your Bible and follow along.)

1. Verses 3-4 make it clear that Paul is challenging you to a flesh contest. Walking after the flesh doesn't necessarily mean chasing women. Some flesh trips can be very productive. Paul claims he's got "better" flesh than you. He can perform better than you can.

2. Since this is the inspired Word of God and Paul states that he has the *best* "old ways," it's true. It means exactly what it says. This man was "Captain Israel!" (Remember, Jesus is not to be considered, as He had no "old ways.")

3. Paul's flesh was generated by *Saul*.

4. Saul's motive for perfecting these patterns for living was to satisfy his need for love. *He sought to get it from God, from others, and from self by meeting up to certain standards (performance).*

5. When Saul got saved, the Bible teaches that he was "crucified with Christ" (Gal. 2:20; see also Rom. 6:6).

6. Saul was "buried with Christ" (Rom. 6:3,4).

7. *Paul (not a resurrected Saul)* was born — created fresh — as a brand new creature in Christ (2 Cor. 5:17).

8. Paul, the *new* spirit man, was born into Saul's former earthsuit (body) after Saul was crucified with Christ.

9. The "old ways," the old program for living, generated by Saul now became Paul's "flesh." It is my personal conviction that this remained in the brain of the earthsuit.

10. Paul states that he abandoned Saul's former method (performance-based acceptance) for getting his need for self-esteem satisfied and opted for God's method (Jesus-based acceptance).

In Philippians 3:9 we see Paul, the new man in Christ, stating that he has scrapped his "old ways" of generating righteousness for "a [different] righteousness not derived from law [*Saul's* standard, which happened to correlate with Mosaic law due to the culture], but based upon the righteousness that is from above through faith in Christ" (author's paraphrase). Make no mistake about it, *perfectionism has its roots in establishing a righteousness of your own based on law — your law.*

It's not carnal for a Christian to be perfectionistic, but Paul's motive for developing it was. Was Paul perfectionistic in his approach to godly living? Yes! But he was liberated from using perfectionism as a means of generating self-acceptance. He generated his self-acceptance through setting his mind on who he now was in Christ — acceptable. He then allowed Christ to live *His* Life through Paul, using Paul's perfectionistic, goal-oriented traits to bring glory to His name on earth, living out His life of agape love.

Will the Real Enemy Please Stand Up?

"Our struggle is not against flesh and blood, but against [the forces of evil]" (Eph. 6:12). I want to caution you as we begin to look at how this all may have worked out in your life that when I point out mistakes made by your parents and peers, you should direct your hostility toward the Biblically identified target, Satan, and not toward your folks. It isn't them you ought to be angry with; it's the Evil One who has worked through your parents to try to destroy you. You want to know why your folks did some of the things they did? Go take a look at what happened to them when they were kids. But let's not get mad at Grandma and Grandpa, either. If you trace all the garbage back to its source, who do you finally wind up with? Satan! He is the one who first deceived, who hates and destroys families. Direct your anger at him — that's Biblical.

Covert Rejection

Anyone can see that little Charlie got overtly rejected by his parents. What most fail to see is that the rejected child's self-image is shaped by his experience so he winds up *feeling* as if his folks are *perfectly justified* in rejecting him. He reasons he'd reject himself, too, if the shoe were on the other foot, because he sees himself as a no-good bum who doesn't deserve to be loved.

But there is a much more subtle form of rejection that's rampant on planet earth. Let's call it "covert rejection." (My friend Charles Solomon has written two excellent books on the subject of rejection, and I highly recommend them both: *The Ins and Out of Rejection* [Harvest House] and *The Rejection Syndrome* [Tyndale].)

In the case of the person who is being overtly rejected, all the cards are up on the table, and by the teen years most children see very well that they are being rejected. In the case of covert rejection, however, most kids never discern what's happening to them. It simply seeps over their personalities like a slowly gathering fog they can't identify, much less verbalize to someone else. The *emotional results are the same* for both types of rejection, though, so the covertly rejected child might say "I *feel* as if they don't love me," whereas the overtly rejected child might say "I *know* nobody loves me."

Examples of Covert Rejection

Perfectionism

If a parent seems to drive himself to perform perfectly in most things he tackles, seems to have perfect performance standards for himself, and insists that his child also perform perfectly, he will unwittingly teach his child that he's inadequate. The child will begin to accept as "fact" the notion, *I can't do anything right! No matter how hard I try, I always foul everything up.* Then his feeler gets stuck, and he begins to feel this way about himself constantly.

The ones who are thirsty for their folks' acceptance adopt the Avis Rent-A-Car posture, "We try harder," and develop into perfectionists themselves. Those who are not, go 180 degrees in the opposite direction, becoming impulsive in their search for acceptance.

When the perfectionist gets saved he will typically become quickly bound by law, *his* law, the law of having to perform perfectly as a Christian in order to accept himself. It's a standard that he's trying to live up to in order to generate and maintain self-acceptance.

No Physical Love

A child who receives no physical love from her folks will *not* learn that *It's very difficult for my folks to demonstrate physical affection*. She will learn *I'm unlovely*. She will then begin to feel unlovely. If Dad avoids holding his little girl on his lap, snuggling her, holding hands while strolling, and so on [all in a healthy way], she will learn about herself in the process, not about Dad. If overt affection from her dad is missing, she has a good chance of developing into an adult female who has hang-ups about relating to males in a physical love relationship, either being sexually promiscuous or perhaps finding it difficult to relate easily to husband, sons, or male friends. When she becomes a born-again believer, this will become a part of her unique version of the flesh. The Evil One will try to control her through these patterns.

Ignore Your Child

Little kids spell love *t-i-m-e*. "Spend time with me" their words and actions cry out. "If you *don't* spend time with me, then whatever you *do* spend time with is worth more to you than I am. Therefore, I am worth less than that is. Therefore, I am *worthless*." It matters not *how* you ignore the child. You can do it by working all the time, golfing all the time, soul-winning all the time, or you can be at home but just never interact with him. The emotional results will usually be the same. He'll feel worthless.

The child doesn't deduce this through a logical reasoning process, but it all comes into him at the gut level nevertheless. We hear it said that it's not the *quantity* of time a parent spends with his child that counts, but the *quality*. (This statement is often heard from the lips of successful, busy men, seldom from women.) You don't get quality time, however, unless you get it by traveling the road of quantity. The intimacy will evolve as a by-product of sharing many good times together. I know of no shortcuts.

How many Christian men and women have I counseled who are either spending their lives in a frantic search to maintain a sense of personal worth, or, at the other extreme, who cannot tolerate success or praise if they do receive it?

I've Got a Better Idea

Some parents are like the Ford Motor Company. No matter how well the child does, they have a habit of suggesting how he could have improved. They rarely praise him. The idea is to consistently give him a "better" way he could have done it after he has already chosen and carried out his own idea. This is an alternative way of producing the same emotional results described above. This communicates to him that he is stupid. If he believes it long enough, his feeler will get stuck. A commonly observed illustration of this is the parent who harps about the only C grade his child receives on his report card while virtually ignoring the As and Bs.

Ridicule

Verbalizing to a child that he is stupid, ugly, clumsy, uncoordinated, lazy, "just like your sorry brother-in-law," and so on gives him solid evidence that he really *is* a loser. Pointing out to a daughter that she'd be "beautiful with a sack over your head" should fix her feeler up just dandy for relating to males later in life. The devil ought to be able to take that kind of garbage and make her either promiscuous or frigid — promiscuous to "prove" her femininity or to obtain male acceptance, or else frigid, convinced that she is totally unfeminine.

Nonverbal Ridicule

Nonverbal ridicule is accomplished by waiting until an appropriate moment, such as when the child hands Dad the wrong screwdriver. The idea is to do things like sighing deeply, rolling the eyes toward the ceiling, slowly wagging the head as if the load is almost too heavy to bear. This produces the same results as overt ridicule and may be even more destructive since it's more subtle. That way the child accepts the total blame for his "stupidity" rather than being able to discern that perhaps he is being mistreated.

No Teaching Time

The mother who never takes time to teach and train her daughter in any of the "womanly" kinds of things—such as baking, sewing, housekeeping, as well as intimate female tasks such as proper hygiene at the onset of menstruation—communicates to her daughter that she is worthless and stupid, that she is not worth her mother's time. In effect, she fails to teach her daughter how to "female." The girl can easily develop into a woman who doesn't feel feminine.

This can also be accomplished by a dad who communicates to his little daughter that he'd wanted her to be a son and so has treated her like a boy. Such a girl often receives her initiation into the world by being given a masculine name at birth. She's whipped before she starts by flunking the physical for acceptance. Often her only "acceptance" from Dad comes by roughhousing with him "like a boy."

The illustration of nonteaching, nonintimacy cited above with the mother-daughter relationship can, of course, be applied to the father-son relationship as well; and a boy who grows up in that situation often develops into a man who feels threatened in his male role.

Overprotection

My friend Chuck Solomon tells a story about an orphaned baby fox that a woman discovered in the country one frigid winter day. She took pity on it, carried it home, bottle fed it, weaned it onto dog food, and taught it tricks such as pushing a button with its nose to fill its water bowl. She loved it almost as if it were a child.

Two years later, she had the most beautiful, full-grown fox in the county. But she began to realize that the time for her to set the fox free to enjoy the fringe benefits of adult fox life had arrived. So, she returned him to the site of their first meeting, and after kissing him good-bye put him out into the woods. As she drove away, her mind was churning, *Oh, how this hurts, she thought. I've poured my life into that fox for two years. I hope he can somehow appreciate that without me he'd be dead.*

But what became of the fox? It was January and getting down to 5 degrees at night. The fox curled up into a ball to try to keep warm. As the cold dawn would break, he could hardly get unballed, he was so stiff. He was hungry and frigid. Something little would scurry past his nose. It was normal fox food, but he didn't know it; he was looking for his dog food. He was thirsty, but knew nothing of searching out the spring a mile away. He was looking for his button to push. In two weeks he was a dead fox!

That woman killed him just as surely as if she'd shot him in the head with a .22. She killed him with what she called "love," but it wasn't love. She didn't really have his best interests at heart [agape]. Her treatment of him kept him from learning how to fox!

People do the same kind of thing to their children. They make all the decisions for them, tell them what to wear, how to stand, how to smile, when they can accept Christ as Savior, and when they can't. They hand pick private schools with teachers who will continue the overprotection process.

When such a kid reaches age twenty-one, his folks say, "All right, Charlie, we've done the very best we could for you, at great personal sacrifice. But the expense was well worth it. Now go out there and face the world! Find yourself a spouse, and live the victorious Christian life. We're expecting great things from you."

The young "adult" then creeps out into the world looking for his dog food bowl and a button to push. He crashes and burns! *He doesn't know how to people.* He's hooked on needing someone to make all his decisions *for* him because he's never been allowed to make any. Physically he's an adult; emotionally he's in elementary school. His feeler's stuck. Color him *feeling* guilty, impotent as a person, and stupid.

Indulgence

Indulgence is one of the most destructive things a parent can do to a child. Its end product is a person with an unbridled, unbroken will who lives with one goal in mind—to take care of Number One. If anything goes wrong, it's never *his* fault. If there are bills to be paid but his church is planning a ski trip to Colorado, he never bats an eye. "Man, I hope there's a new snow cover when we get there" is all he says.

This problem of indulgence seems to be escalating, and I believe it's because we have so many working mothers. Admittedly it's sometimes necessary for a mother to work outside the home, but often the motive is TV sets and boats. The working parents arrive home at 5:30 with Johnny in tow from the day-care center. Everyone's tired, and the child misbehaves. The folks don't want to discipline him, so they let him get away with things too much. Through this process, he becomes the acting head of the house. He runs things *his* way. He is Lord of the Family Ring.

Being a Christian means among other things that I submit myself to God's authority over me. I agree to let Him establish His Kingdom inside me. I let Him sit in my chair. But the indulged person often has great difficulty submitting to *any* authority. Unless he agrees totally with that authority, in which case *he* still remains in control. Color him feeling rebellious.

Stonewalling

Parents will often bottle up their emotions and give their children few outward signs of how they're feeling. It complicates matters all the more if a given parent is a quiet person who communicates only with "Yes," "No," "Maybe," and similarly uninformative answers. The child of such a parent, because of his need for acceptance, will begin to try to read Mom by Braille. He'll crank out his feelings antenna and search for emotional evidence that he's making it with her. He constantly checks his emotions as *the* barometer of truth that determines how his mom is reacting to him.

Females are especially vulnerable to this, because the Lord has constructed them to be intuitive folks to begin with. The female has the ability to arrive at a conclusion via a mysterious inner "knowing" and be right on target—much more so than a male. Thus, girls can be deceived into working their intuition overtime, and it results in overly depending on their emotions as a valid indicator of "truth."

Performance-Based Acceptance

I have attempted to describe briefly some of the major mistakes that may have been made by your parents and could have resulted in your growing into an adult Christian who has a lot of difficulty making the Christian life work. But I believe we have yet to hit upon the devil's biggest weapon. His most effective technique, visible in epidemic proportions, is "performance-based love," or "performance-based acceptance," which I'll sometimes refer to as PBA.

It works like this. If you perform (act) as I want you to, I'll accept you; if you don't, I'll reject you. In other words, I realize that I possess something that you need — love. So I'm going to use my "supply" to control you.

The youngest of our four sons is named Wade. Suppose I caught him lying to me when he was eight. Watch me blow it as I interact with him. "All right, Wade, you lied to me!" This is okay, so far. I'm nailing his poor performance. "If there's anything I can't stand, it's a *liar*." Oh, oh; I've ceased to deal with *performance* and have switched to criticizing the *performer*. "And your mother can't stand liars either! We promised each other thirty years ago that we'd never tolerate a liar in this house, but it looks like we've got our first liar! And God hates liars, too! 'All liars shall have their place in the hell of fire!' I'll show you what we do to liars around here! We spank 'em! You get into that bedroom, you liar!" And I lay it on him.

Rear Wade this way for several years, and then interview him at age fifteen. If you could get him to open up to you, this is what he'd say. "I *feel* like Dad can't stand *me* because of the way I *act*. Neither can Mom. She can't stand to be around me. It's just this *feeling* I've got. I know it's true. And I *feel* like God is mad at me most of the time, too, because of the way I act. Oh, I see all those verses in the Bible about how much God loves me, but I just don't *feel* that way about my relationship with Him. And you know, I don't blame any of them, because I don't like me, either! Fact is, if they *did* start to act like they loved me, I'd think they'd lost their marbles."

See? *His feeler would be stuck on rejection.* That's the result of performance-based acceptance. I don't want to do that to Wade, and neither did your folks want to reject their children that way.

That's the devil's work. But I've got to deal with Wade's lying. How do I accomplish this without destroying his personhood?

Reject Performance, Not Performer

It's really pretty simple once you see it. You deal with the performance, not with the performer. Here's how I should handle the lying: "All right, Wade Gillham, you lied to me." I'm rejecting performance. "And if there's one thing I can't stand, it's *lying*." I'm still rejecting performance. "And your mother can't stand it either. Thirty years ago, we swore that there was one thing we would never allow in our house, and that's *lying*. We never have, and we don't intend to begin with you. And God can't stand lying, either. He hates it! Christ died because of stuff like that!" Now, have I said anything about Wade? No, I'm talking about what he *did*, not about *him*. I'm dealing with his performance, not his person.

Now Deal With Person, Not Performance

I could continue: "Now, Wade, if I didn't love you, I'd let you go ahead and lie. I'd indulge you and let you generate a big, green highway for lying to people to get your needs met. But I won't fail you like that. That would be rejecting you. I love you too much to do that. So, I'm going to help you with your problem. You get into that bedroom. I'm going to spank you for lying to me." Can you see that the very act of disciplining Wade will now be a demonstration of my commitment to him and my love for him? "Those whom the Lord loves He disciplines" (Heb. 12:6).

If we interview Wade at age fifteen after having been reared under this system, he'd say, "Dad can't stand the way I *act* sometimes, but he sure does love *me*. Mom's the same way. Sometimes the things I *do* really bug her, but there's no doubt in my mind that she loves *me*. And God is displeased with some of my behavior, too, but this one thing I know. He loves *me*. Hey, *I* don't always like the way I *act*, either. I'm working on that, but I accept myself. I like *me*." Do you see the difference?

PBA—Satan's Chief Tool on Earth

Every religion from Mormonism to voodoo is based on PBA, humanity's seeking acceptance from God by earning it. Christianity, however, is *relationship*, not religion. God reaches out to us with grace (unmerited favor) through Jesus Christ's finished work. This relationship is not for sale. Jesus bought it with His life. It cannot be earned through PBA. You don't earn a gift, you gratefully accept it.

The world system, on the other hand, is based totally on PBA, whether you're trying to get the acceptance of peers in the jungles of the Amazon or the jungles of Harlem; whether you're reared in a Mafia member's home or a pastor's home. Performance is the name of the game. Perform well enough and you can earn your love supply out of your environment, even in your church.

One of the best examples I can offer in our culture is the school system. Now, I'm not setting out to condemn the schools, but let's face it, they weren't handed down from Mount Sinai. They are part of the world. Even the Christian schools are not exempt from PBA.

PBA in the Classroom

I'm going to use Bill, my number three son, as "Exhibit A." I saved some of his first-grade papers to illustrate my point about PBA in our schools. He's a grown man now, a delightful brother who's a Christian musician. Illustration 2.1 depicts one of his spelling papers.

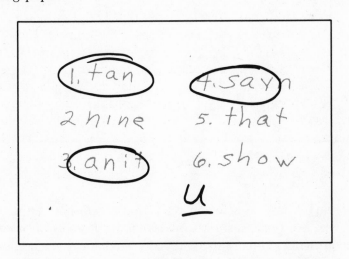

Illustration 2.1

Now, let's say that I decide I need to go up to the school to discuss Bill's progress (or lack of it) with his teacher. I say, "Ma'am, I see here that Bill's given it six shots, and he's got three right and three wrong, which got him a grade of U. But what about this word 'nine'? He got that one right, but you didn't say anything about that one. How come?"

She might say, "Now, Dr. Gillham, you've got to understand something. It's not Bill's handling of the word 'nine' that we're concerned with this year. He's already got that one whipped. It's the word 'ten' he's having trouble with 'cause he's from Oklahoma. He calls it 'tan.' Now, that's a problem." Her whole focus is on drawing attention to errors, not on encouraging small signs of progress.

Here's another paper that's not Bill's. It was given to me by the mother of a seven-year-old boy. He produced it for a creative writing assignment (see Illustration 2.2).

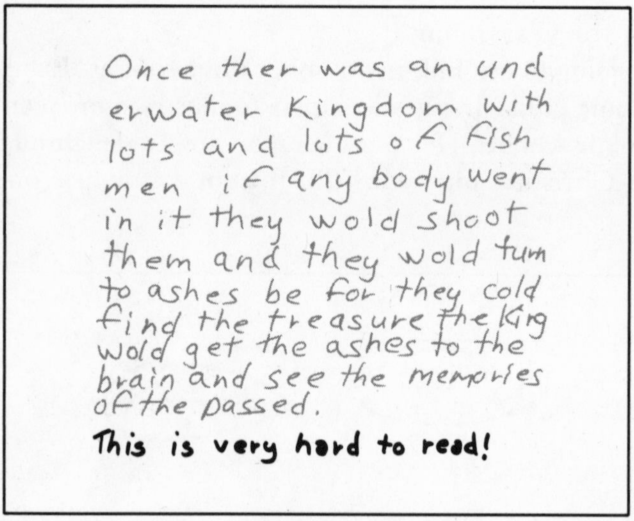

Once ther was an und
erwater Kingdom with
lots and lots of fish
men if any body went
in it they wold shoot
them and they wold tum
to ashes be for they cold
find the treasure the King
wold get the ashes to the
brain and see the memories
of the passed.

This is very hard to read!

Illustration 2.2

I don't know how extensively you've studied human intelligence, but this is a smart cookie! We want to do what we can to encourage a kid like this. Did you see what his teacher put on his paper, however? "This is very hard to read!" Thud. Instead of encouraging his talent, she put him down. She passed up an opportunity to edify and build up, and he's going to take it as a personal inadequacy.

Now back to my Willie for one more example. In the paper below, you can see that the teacher has discovered a severe case of the short lower case e's. She marked every one of them wrong! (See Illustration 2.3.)

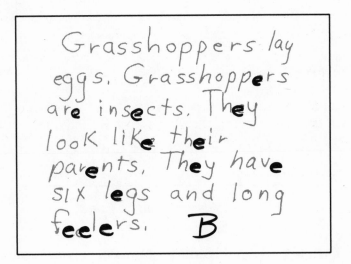

Illustration 2.3

Let's say that I decide it's time to go back up to see the teacher again, and I take Bill's paper along. I say, "Now, Ma'am, I see you've given Bill a B because he's blown it with his little e's there, but what about this 'o' in the word Grasshopper? That's a pretty good looking 'o.' And how about that 'l' in lay? That's nice and straight, and you didn't say anything nice about that."

And she'd say something like this to me, "Now, Dr. Gillham. I'm beginning to gain some insight into your son's problem. Let's take it from the top again. We're not interested in your boy's o's and l's. He's got those down pat. But if we're ever going to stamp the ignorance out of him, we've got to get him straightened out on his e's." You see, her mentality is that in order to help him, she's got to find something wrong that he's doing and then straighten him out.

Now, to show you I've got this teacher pegged right, look at this one. She's scored it 100, but messy. She can't get him on math today, so she's going to nail him on cleanliness! (See Illustration 2.4.)

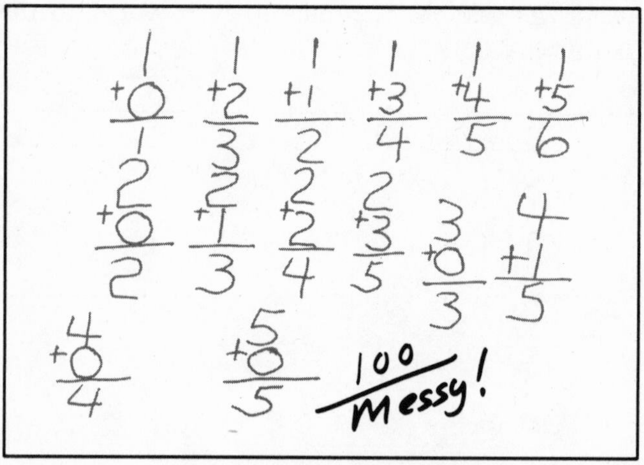

Illustration 2.4

If a teacher carries this critical attitude far enough, she could fix it so there's no way he can win. And if his need to please is high enough, if the person doing this rejection number on him is a high priority person in his life, what's he learning? Is he learning *Man, what an old bat!* No, he's learning, *I'm stupid. I can't do anything right. I wish I were different.*

I don't mean to pick on this teacher. I'm hammering the system—not the school system, the world system. It's designed to destroy, especially the weak ones, the very ones upon whom the Lord Jesus has compassion. And *we* do it to them. We do it in our own homes, to our own spouses and kids! I managed my own family this way for years. Praise God, He turned me around, but more about that later when I discuss my unique version of the flesh.

Encourage One Another

What's the alternative to PBA in the classroom setting? Here's another paper from a real teacher's class (see Illustration 2.5).

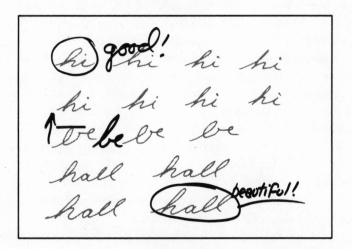

Illustration 2.5

This teacher is simply trying to discover the best thing the child has done on the paper and comment on it. It's not flattery. The Word teaches not to do that, that it's hollow. She's just trying to encourage, to find something she can do to edify the people around her.

Does that mean a teacher should never tell a student he's doing something wrong? Of course not. But you have to earn the right to do it. Look at this paper (see Illustration 2.6):

Illustration 2.6

You see, the teacher has encouraged the child with "good" and "beautiful." Her positive attitude toward him has earned her the right to say, "Oh, by the way, George, your lower case b's are too short. Here's a model for you to imitate next time." How do you suppose he's going to respond to that kind of encouragement? The same way you would!

That's a picture of Jesus Christ. What if He had said to Peter at the first opportunity, "Get thee behind me, Satan!" Scratch one prospective disciple! The guy never would have joined up. It would have been "Jesus and the eleven." But no, He loved him in obvious ways, thus earning the right to love him yet another way by punching him out. Sure, He got tough with people at times, but they *needed* it.

Jesus-Based Acceptance

One of the best-kept secrets in Christianity is that God accepts us. True, He can't stand our sinful acts, but He loves *us*. He doesn't have us on performance-based acceptance; He has us on *Jesus-based acceptance*. If you have accepted Jesus as your Lord and Savior, the Father has accepted you completely. Performance has nothing whatever to do with it. Performance is important to God, yes, but it has to do with winning His *approval*, not His acceptance. It has to do with hearing Him say, "Well done, good and faithful servant" one day at the Judgment Seat of Christ, but nothing to do with hearing Him say, "I accept you as My beloved child" (John 1:12).

You can be the greatest performer on the block at keeping God's standards, and you'll still be totally rejected by God if you are unsaved. One of the major purposes of those standards (the Ten Commandments, the Sermon on the Mount, etc.), is to frustrate you to the point where you'll see that there's no way you're ever going to earn His acceptance. You've got to change methods. You've got to come to the Father through *Christ's* perfection, just as He said.

To demonstrate how deeply entrenched Satan has made the performance-based acceptance syndrome, consider this Biblically-based illustration. On a one-to-ten scale, where ten is the best, put a number on how well you accept yourself, your spouse, and your kids, assuming all are born again. Let's suppose you selected a five for yourself. You're saying that you still have five additional points to climb before you can accept yourself perfectly.

But God accepts you perfectly in Christ already. God doesn't grade on a one-to-ten scale; He grades pass-fail. His acceptance of you and me is not contingent on our performance; but on what we have done with Jesus Christ's performance *for* us. If you have surrendered to Jesus as Lord and Savior, then God has already accepted you completely. He couldn't love or accept you more if you had never sinned. And He'll never love or accept you less no matter how often you *do* sin.

Actually, any Christian who accepts himself or any other believer at less than ten has higher standards than God! He sees himself and his loved ones falling far short of the standard for acceptance. This person is using performance as the criterion for acceptance. God, however, uses Christ's finished work for us as the criterion for acceptance. Thus, any Christian who's striving for acceptance is fighting a battle that's already been won.

(For additional help in identifying your unique version of the flesh, see the "Flesh Inventory" on pages 223-224.)

Questions for Further Study

1. In Philippians 3:3-9, Paul elaborates on his unique version of the flesh. How was his flesh developed?

2. What are some of the insights you have gained thus far concerning the flesh, and what has God's Spirit pointed out to you concerning your version of the flesh? Hint: take special note of how you get your need for love and self-love met.

3. What is necessary to be accepted by God?

THREE

HOW ANABEL AND I GOT INTO OUR FIX

Anabel, my precious wife who's trusted God's grace to take her through the deep water of being married to me, approached her wedding day with great anticipation. With a track record of twenty-two years of success at playing Lord of the Ring, she was confident of her ability to make it fly. Other women seemed to be able to perform well enough in their marriages. A lot of them seemed happy and content. If they could handle it, so could she. After all, hadn't she always been able to handle life?

She could learn how to cook to please her husband. She could mend clothing. She could redecorate rooms and plan the grocery shopping. She could learn to meet her husband's sexual needs. She could do it. She had *self*-confidence.

After the honeymoon was over, however, life settled into the routine of "How can we plug my electric razor and her hair curler into one outlet?" "When are you going to be through at the lavatory? I've got to be to work by 8:00 you know!" "Would you *please* not run the washer when I'm in the shower. I swear, the next time you do that to me, you're going to regret it!"

Things weren't going the way she'd planned. What *could* she do? Of course! That's it! She'd regroup and try harder. Knowing that hot biscuits are one of my favorite dishes and wanting desperately to start the day off on the right foot so it would be a *good* day, Anabel was up bright and early making delectable aromas flow from the kitchen.

In came Big Daddy with his "red pencil" nicely sharpened to begin his day by checking his wife's performance. "Biscuits for breakfast! I believe you let 'em get a little bit too brown this morning, Sugar." I ate half the platter and left for work.

Anabel was a bit disappointed by this. Not exactly the response or the gratitude she'd hoped for. But it was nothing she couldn't shake off. And after all, she could try harder next time, right? She had learned through many years of success at playing Lord of the Ring that she could do better the next time. There's always a next time, and she always does better the next time. She'd learned that. She was capable. She could do it.

So, she tried again the next day, this time turning the timer down thirty seconds to be sure they didn't get too brown.

"Biscuits again!" said Big Daddy, his fingers still red from sharpening his pencil.

"Yes! All for you this morning, Dear, to show you how much I love you!"

"Uh, I believe you took 'em out of the oven a little early this morning, Honey. They look a little too light." I ate half the platter again and left for work.

And then I recall a time, very early in our marriage. We were still living in our little honeymoon apartment. One Saturday morning I took Anabel by the hand and led her into our little living room. I held her hand, sighed a bit at what I felt I had to do for her own good, looked her in the eye, and gently said, "Honey, I wish you would learn to do just *one* thing well." Can you believe it? I ought to have been whipped with a wet rope!

Today, the pain being history, Anabel says, "Of course, things like that crushed me. But I'll tell you one thing. It didn't destroy me. I came out of it pulling myself up by my bootstraps, vowing that I would improve. Next time I'd do better! I can do better! I've learned that I can always do better!"

In this chapter, I want to show you Anabel's and my flesh patterns and how they came to be. You'll also see how two very different kinds of flesh tried to coexist in one family. I trust that our example will give you insight into your own situation.

There was the time we were in the car heading for a square dance on Friday night. It was our big night out after a week's work. Anabel was so excited. She'd tried hard to look pretty to please her husband. But by this time, I had developed new weapons. Whereas before I had been attacking her performance, I now began to attack her person. You may be able to try harder to improve your performance, but how can you try harder when your identity is being attacked?

I directed my attention over to my sweet, twenty-seven-year-old wife of six years and said, "I can't imagine anyone wanting to square dance with you." Right out of the blue! Why, if her dad had known what she was living with, he'd have rung my chimes, and I would have deserved it.

One night I found Jesus as I watched Billy Graham on television. It was his first nationwide telecast from Madison Square Garden in 1957. Many things changed about my life after my conversion, but that hostile, chip-on-my-shoulder attitude in my home didn't change one whit. I call it being "wormy." I went right on with the red pencil routine, only by this time we had some sons, and they came in for their share of it as well.

Here's a typical episode. It's grocery shopping time. Anabel parks in our drive and toots the horn for me to help carry in the bags. By this time in our marriage I had made a shoulder holster for my red pencil, so I could whip it out in a flash. Wyatt Earp had nothing on me. Oh, I was fast, real fast.

So now in the kitchen I'm helping unpack the grocery sacks, and I say, "Del Monte green beans? How come?"

"Well, they're the best. I just hate to get one of those cheap brands and have it ruin a meal. I don't mind paying a little extra for top quality."

"Listen. Sure Fine green beans are good enough for this family, and they're a nickel cheaper. Hey, we don't drive a Cadillac! We're Chevy people. It upsets me that you're so careless with your spending. You're getting to where you do things like this more and more. I wish you'd cut it out!"

Stung by such an unexpected outburst when she considered herself to be trying so hard to please, she begins to get a little down about the whole thing. But after a few hours of struggling with feelings of failure, she shakes it off and determines that she'll do better the next time.

The next time she has green beans on her shopping list, then, she makes sure to get, you guessed it, a six-pack of Sure Fines. *This will please Bill*, she reasons. *He wants me to get Sure Fines*. But guys, she failed to notice a very important event that was taking place across town at Safeway. Del Monte's were on sale for six cents off! So what should I do as we're unpacking the sack and I become aware of this horrible case of poor steward-ship! She has just squandered an extra penny per can for beans of inferior quality! What should I do, men? "Lord?" I prayed. "The woman You gave me has blown it! I try and try to help her clean up her act, but she just can't do anything right. I guess I'm going to have to tell her."

I told her, and I told her, and I told her, and I took the finest thing outside of salvation that the Lord has ever given me — a person who loved me enough to give herself to me until death, a person who busted herself trying to be the best wife she could possibly be — and I almost destroyed her. I did it with this thing that lies between my teeth. I reduced her nearly to the point of suicide.

Why couldn't I change? After all, I was born again. Anabel and I were trying our best to make Christ the center of our home. I was one of the leading soul-winners in my church; I worked like a Trojan, conducted jail services every Sunday after-noon, and attended church Sunday morning and night, and Wednesday night, too. I read my Bible and prayed. But when the door to my own house closed behind me, I was a destroyer, and I couldn't stop.

What was the problem? I was "walking after the flesh," my unique version of it. How did I get that way? What could have possibly happened to me during my formative years to turn me into such a tyrant? I know exactly what happened.

My Flesh

I dare not challenge you to come to the end of your flesh trip without first having come to the end of mine. That certainly is not to say that I never fall back and walk according to the flesh, but it certainly *is* to say that I experience 95 percent better vic-tory than I did before I held a good funeral for that way of life.

As each Christian's unique version of the flesh is heavily, although not totally, shaped by his formative years, I'm going to have to talk about my relationship with my mom and dad. They're with the Lord now, but I want you to understand some-thing at the start. I love Mom and Pop. I'm glad they were my folks. I wouldn't trade my heritage for anyone's. The way they interacted with me is a vitally important part of my pilgrimage with Jesus. Had it been different, I would not have traveled this route, and, thus, I would not have fit into the niche the Lord had in mind for me.

When I showed up on planet earth, the Lord put me into a male earthsuit. My dad was a Presbyterian pastor, and I was the eldest son. Now, ladies, I am about to make some statements that will come off as chauvinistic. Please don't write me off as that. I readily confess that I *used* to be, but I'm not now. I am a new man in Christ, and I have overcome that portion of the flesh. So please hang in there with me.

According to the manufacturer's instructions (the Bible), my folks' marriage was upside down. Mom was "lifing out" more of the husband's role in that she was definitely the stronger of the two personalities. When decisions were to be made, she made them. If I wanted to go play with the kid down the block, there was no point in asking my dad, because he would respond, "Go ask your mom." This held true for major as well as minor decisions and Mom often emphasized her position with a marked increase in decibels. We often said she was "strong as an acre of garlic."

Pop, meanwhile, was "lifing out" more of a wifely role in that he totally submitted to Mom. When Mom said "frog," he jumped. Pop avoided decisions. If he ever got pinned down on an issue, he'd say, "I'm out of it," and he'd split. We facetiously told him that we were going to put this epitaph on his tombstone: "I'm sure 'nuff out of it!" Although Pop had many godly traits, in this one he gave me a nonbiblical male role model that blocked my ability to generate male self-esteem by playing Lord of the Ring.

Mom wanted to make me into a pansy-preacher's-boy type. I had long hair until I was five years old, and no boys had long hair back when I was a kid. She also had me dressed out in knickers. I got my first long pants when I was nine years old. And since all the other boys wore overalls, I didn't exactly fit into the culture.

Striving for Self-Acceptance

A little boy has many needs, one of which is to *feel* like a male — like he belongs as a male. It's going to cause him problems if he begins to feel like a misfit. He'll have trouble accepting himself (there's that word again).

What do I mean when I say a boy needs to feel like a boy? Well, a five-year-old boy needs to believe he can throw a rock straighter than a five-year-old girl. He needs to feel he can handle lizards and toads and the girls will squeal with horror at such "strength and daring." They'll shriek. "Ugh, they'll give you warts on your hands!"

And he'll say, "Aw, rain on that. Let 'em give me warts clear up. to my elbows. See if I care!"

That's a boy for you, right? And you know, I still have a lot of that in me. I'm not into toads any more, but I like to feel that Anabel sees me as strong; that she feels she can depend on me; that I have wise counsel; that she doesn't have to carry the load of making decisions alone concerning problems that arise in the family. In short, I guess I need to feel as though she sees me as her *husband*, not as a little boy.

Now, as a child, Mom represented all femininity to me. So, if I was ever to accept myself as male, I had to ultimately see myself as being stronger than Mom! That looked like climbing Mount Everest! In addition to this intimidation, my male role model was demonstrating behavior contrary to God's plan, so I had no help, no markers along the path of life to aid me in learning how to "male."

Three Roads

The Holy Spirit has shown me through counseling with hundreds and hundreds of people that a boy in an environment such as I have described will respond in one of three ways, although he can combine them.

First, he may become homosexual. He may be so intimidated by his environment that he will come to see the normal male role that God intended him to walk in as impossible. He literally gives up on *being* male and does a 180 degree turn away from it. As Lord of his Ring, he opts to get his need for love met the "best" way he can (with a lot of help from the Evil One). This did not happen to me, although it surely could have. I have counseled many men who were born anew, but who had great struggles with homosexual temptation because they were products of an upside-down marriage.

Second, he may become passive. He just *semi* gives up on

being male and begins to journey through life passively getting his needs met by taking whatever acceptance crumbs the women and stronger males will sweep to him from their tables. His motto becomes, "I'm anybody's dog who will hunt with me." He's afraid to have an opinion because he *feels* that people who disagree will reject him. He can't stand this, so he defers to their power to get his need for love satisfied.

Tragically, this passes for godliness in some Christians' perception when, in fact, it's just chicken flesh. This man operates out of fear of men, and his motive is his quest for love. We've got to stop electing this type of man to positions of authority in the Church until he gets victory over the flesh. His lifestyle of riding the fence on issues is not Christ in Him; it's the flesh.

I see some of this in me. I have struggled with this aspect of my flesh patterns, especially around strong males. I have victory over this now through understanding who I now am in Christ, but it's still a temptation for me.

Third, he can go the macho route. He "sucks it up" and says to himself, "I *will* be male. I can *do* it. I desperately *need* to see myself as male. I've *got* to make it."

This is the route I took. I rebelled against my mom's dominance and my dad's passivity. I tried awfully hard to "overcome" my past by proving *to myself* that I was male.

Self-Help City

What could a young boy do to help himself feel more like a male? Well, the tack I took was to be vulgar and profane. I took pride in being foul-mouthed, even as a small child. And it paid off. It was viewed as macho by my peers. It wouldn't work now because women are also vulgar and profane, but back in my youth it worked great.

Move Over, John Wayne!

Okay, let's move me into the high school years. What could I do at this level to prove to myself that I was male? I had to keep adding more tools to my toolbox as I got older, see? My "ring" was getting more complex. For one thing, I could become an athlete. In the little Oklahoma community where Anabel and I grew up (Poteau), we spelled athlete "football player." So I went out for football. There was just one problem: my earthsuit. It was 5 feet 2 inches tall, and it weighed 110 pounds. It had a size 13 neck and no hair on its legs. If you live inside an earthsuit like that and you've got to make that thing play football, your soul is in trouble! But I was out there playing, scared to death. I *had* to play; I *needed* what I perceived it could do for me, which was to help me accept myself better.

Move Over, Clark Gable!

What else could a high school boy do to build up his masculine image? Well, you could seduce the women. But wait a minute. Back there in Chapter 1, we learned that a small child learns about himself from the feedback he gets from others. And in our house, nobody ever kissed anybody. So at age fifteen, the kid had virgin lips! Mom didn't even let the dog lick me. So how did I feel about myself? Unkissy. Oh, man, how I longed to kiss the women, but somehow I couldn't bring myself to even try. My feeler was stuck.

You can readily see that I was not into sex. While I was desiring to be sexually active at level ten, I was intimidated by the thoughts that I would be rejected or that I would fail, and that was a ten. Thus, all my sexual experiences took place at the fantasy level. When I ultimately got saved, these flesh patterns were going to haunt me as I tried to walk in a godly manner. I was going to pay a heavy price for striving for acceptance as a male.

"Vengeance is Mine," Saith the Threatened Male

Somewhere along the way, I discovered a tool that I added to my tool chest and that proved to be very effective in helping me accept myself. It was more a weapon than a tool. I directed it at the people who were the major threat to my self-acceptance as a male. Who were those people? Women, especially strong ones. They instantly triggered in me all the frustrations I had experienced since childhood. If I could just get them out of my life, if I could destroy them, that would give me a feeling of superiority, of conquest. I couldn't do it sexually, as I have already explained, but there was another way. I could do it with my tongue.

As a male, God made me more of a logical thinker than your typical female. She tends to be more of an intuitive thinker, more of a sensitive person. If I came in contact with a strong gal in high school, I would use sarcasm and invective on her. I would catch her in a group setting, rarely one-on-one, and make fun of her—ridicule the way she looked, the way she sang, the way she acted, the new zit she was trying to hide on her neck, or whatever—until she broke from the stress. You see, she couldn't fight that way. Her sensitivity would disarm her, whereas I was insulated with indifference to her hurt. I could laugh off her retorts and hurl double the insults back in her face. She would break and begin to cry or scream at me. At this point it was usually difficult for me to keep a straight face, because inside I was experiencing glee. I had won!

Sad, isn't it? But look around you at the millions of marriages, both Christian and non-Christian, that fit this mold. A strong gal is married to a threatened guy, and open warfare is the order of the day.

I am not proud of what I just told you about myself. Quite the contrary. But do you see a picture of a seventeen-year-old boy struggling for self-esteem? Do you see that's how he played Lord of the Ring in an effort to generate and maintain self-esteem? And when I got saved, all this garbage was going to become my "old ways," my flesh that I would have to struggle against.

My "Completer"

As my flesh was being formed along the lines I've just described, Anabel, my sweet wife whom the Father gave to me, was also having her flesh shaped. I'll let her tell the story in her own words.

> Bill was having lunch recently with Harold, a friend who had been my classmate at dear old Poteau High. Harold was a very competent, aggressive student—an athlete. As they were discussing years gone by, Harold made this observation: "You know, Bill, Anabel and I were in the same class when we were growing up there in Poteau. I had one goal. That was to beat her in at least one common undertaking. I never did."
>
> I am one of two daughters of Marcus and Jean Hoyle. One of the most tender and intimate moments that I remember with

my beloved daddy was sitting out on the back steps one evening. I was between his legs, and he had his arms around my
neck. Mother had just undergone a hysterectomy. Dad, in a
very gentle, poignant voice, said to me, "You know, Honey,
you're the only little boy I'll ever have."

Now, I can't remember trying to be a tomboy to please my
daddy. But I was the ultimate in tomboys! There were a lot of
boys in our neighborhood, and they would congregate in our
yard to play. If we played cowboys and Indians, you can be
very sure that Anabel was the chief. If we played cops and rob-
bers, I was the sheriff. I even remember Daddy tying ropes in
the mulberry tree so that I could be Tarzan. And neither of
them ever said anything like, "Anabel, when are you going to
grow up and start acting like a little lady?"

I was playing Lord of the Ring, forming patterns for male-
female interaction and relationships to get their acceptance (I
thought) and generate self-esteem. My patterns were not very
acceptable ones to the males.

At Howard Elementary School, of course, the most important subject of the day was recess. This particular time, we
were running races down under the hill. I can remember telling
Mother and Daddy at the supper table how I had beaten Mer-
vin McConnell in races that day. I'm sure they responded
favorably. But that was not the ultimate. The ultimate was the
time when I told them that I had beaten Joe Harold West in
races. Why? Well, Joe Harold was my boyfriend! Sigh.

Eighth grade. Everyone anticipated the annual trek up
Cavanal Mountain in the spring. I had a new boyfriend,
Robert Henry Kendrick. Of course, he didn't know it, and I
had to impress him. How was I going to do that? Why, the
same way that I had been impressing boys since the days in our
backyard. I was going to do whatever he did as well as he did it
or better! Robert Henry was definitely the "leader of the pack."
But guess who was by his warm side all the way up the mountain? Anabel. I still remember the two of us sitting on the big
rocks that overlook Poteau Valley. I don't remember verbatim
what he said, but it was something to this effect: "You're quite a
mountain climber." He had noticed me. My heart sang! But
my joy was short-lived. He *carried* Joan Caldwell down the
mountain because she had a blister on her poor little foot!

I began to see things in the movies about this time that
made a definite impression on me. Names that you may not

recognize—Lauren Bacall and Humphrey Bogart—were my stars. I *liked* what I saw. One movie had a profound effect on my life, "Mrs. Miniver," with Greer Garson and Walter Pidgeon. Why? Well, I saw two people as man and wife who had fun together; they respected each other; they were tender and loving; they were kind and considerate. I wasn't seeing this in my home. Mother and Dad had a stormy relationship. I started thinking, *Maybe this being a woman isn't all that bad.* I began to see that I was something very special, something very beautiful—a woman.

But the patterns I'd developed for interacting with males and that Bill had developed for interacting with females were going to lead us into a self-destructive marriage.

Self-Destructive Marriage

As you can see, Anabel and I developed very different kinds of flesh. During our courtship, however, I was careful to keep all my undesirable, critical-toward-women behavior under wraps, especially with Anabel. I treated her like a queen. You see, she is a beauty, and it fed my masculinity needs to be number one in her life. But after the marriage, when I got her into the castle with the drawbridge up, I began to show my true self. This loving, caring, tender, compassionate, attentive, young man became sarcastic, hateful, critical, indifferent, self-centered, self-indulgent, and downright mean at times. I began to pour all my years of pent-up frustration against strong women out onto one of the dearest women God ever created. I was a strong woman hater.

Someone may be wondering why I would be dumb enough to marry a strong woman. Why not choose one who would submit to my every wish?

Remember the rattlesnake illustration back in Chapter 1 that demonstrates how your emotions get stuck? Well, since I had spent twenty-three years doubting my masculinity and my ability to have it all together as a male, as a leader, how did I feel by now? Inadequate. Oh, I *wanted* to be the strong leader at home, but I didn't feel I could do it. I felt more like a boy. I felt I needed a combination wife and mother. My feeler was stuck on about an eight. So I married a woman who would run the ship, discipline the kids, manage the money, make wise decisions, and so on.

I married according to my feeler, in other words. But bless her heart, Anabel had not married my dad. She had married someone who was out to destroy her. I didn't know this. I didn't lie in bed at night and plot it. I didn't know what was driving me. All I knew was that I *felt* frustrated, threatened and unhappy with myself. It all looked hopeless.

Here's the way the cycle went. I stayed frustrated with myself, say, at level five. Show me someone who's frustrated, and I'll show you someone who's hostile. I had a deep need to ease that frustration. As a Christian, I knew it was not of God and wanted to overcome it, yet the hostility sat in there like a bomb waiting to detonate. (Some Christians have "implode" flesh, some have "explode." I have explode flesh.)

Anabel, meanwhile, kept doing things that irritated me, and I cut her down to size with my tongue. She, laboring under the burden of performance-based acceptance, made like Avis and tried harder. Stung by her husband's criticism of her performance, she felt rejected.

Remember, though, that Anabel also felt *self*-rejection. She couldn't love herself as well as she could had she not received this negative feedback on her performance. What was her old, fleshly remedy for the situation? Try to improve! So she doubled her effort, and more often than not, she made improvements on her already yeoman production.

This in turn threatened me even more, as it was a continual reminder of my own inability to accept myself as male. Her competency increased my self-rejection since I was being "outdone" by a woman, and my hostility accelerated. What was my way of getting relief? Strike out at the "cause," Anabel.

Being rejected again, she tried to do better (to get her need for love met), and the cycle began again. We were two people walking after their unique versions of the flesh.

Thorns in the Flesh

In 2 Corinthians 12, Paul speaks of having known a man who was lifted up into heaven. He then says that he, Paul, was given a thorn in the flesh to keep him humble. Most would agree that the man who was lifted to heaven was Paul, else why would he have been given a thorn to keep him humble?

It is irrelevant to our discussion to speculate on what the thorn was. The emphasis in the passage is not on the thorn, but on its purpose. It was to make Paul's flesh trip (pride) unproductive.

The Lord has designed your marriage so that each of you completes the other. There have been many books written enumerating the positive ways spouses complement or complete one another. But I'll bet that if you examine your situation honestly, you will discover that your spouse's flesh in some way is a "thorn" in your flesh. There will be something about his or her flesh patterns that bugs yours or makes it unproductive for you to use them. God's purpose is that you be broken from walking after the flesh, and He has lovingly given you a "thorn" to motivate you to abandon the flesh trip.

Take Anabel and me, for example. One of my eight-lane, green highways is that supercritical tongue. One of Anabel's is a supersensitivity to any evaluative comments about her performance. Our omniscient God left those in there at our salvation for us to "work out our own salvation" (mature in Christ; see Phil. 2:12, 13). He could have zapped them out, but He left them there for us to work on as a learning and maturing activity so Christ could be glorified through our victory.

What if God had married me to a leather-skinned woman whom I could bounce invective off of all day long and she'd keep dishing it right back at me? She'd finish with, "Okay, boy, it's Cheerios for you until you get your act together!" Why, I'd redouble my efforts to come up with innovative ways to destroy her. My flesh trip would actually escalate under such conditions. But no. God married me to a gal who can't even tolerate it if I suggest she buy a different brand of green beans. She'd go through a half day of down time over such things. Brother, that'll motivate you to beg God to help you clean up your act.

And how about Anabel? What if she were married to a guy who would never say anything evaluative to her? She could just go through her Christian life sheltered from ever having to deal with her unique version of the flesh. If she got "hurt" at Sunday school, they'd just change churches.

Instead, however, the Lord gave Anabel and me to each other for keeps. Our toothbrushes are in the same glass. There's no way we can run from one another. We have to stay hitched and "make no provision for the flesh" (Rom. 13:14). We are learning how to let Christ live through us to overcome the flesh. And praise God, it's working! We are making progress to His glory.

How about you? Are you receiving the thorns you *need* for dealing with your flesh, or are you murmuring at God about them? All murmuring will get you is a season pass on the wilderness merry-go-round. You've got to hold a funeral for that kind of behavior.

Questions for Further Study

1. What do you see God doing in your life to motivate you toward dealing with the fleshly patterns you have recognized?

2. Why does God not erase all the old flesh patterns at salvation, total commitment, or some other significant single encounter with Him?

3. If you have USDA Choice Flesh, by and large, and find yourself running into one brick wall after the next, what is one of the potential reasons for this?

FOUR

AN "OLD MAN" IN A NEW EARTHSUIT

Earlier in the book, I pointed out that the perspective and thinking of small children is totally self-centered. All they care about is getting their own needs met and having their own way. And has it ever occurred to you that they don't need to be taught to be that way? Nobody has to instruct a child to pursue his needs regardless of the consequences to others; we have to teach the opposite over and over. Likewise, nobody has to train a one-year-old to defy Mommy and throw a tantrum when she wants him to take a nap; it just comes naturally.

As you continue to read, keep in mind that we are all self-centered. We are all lost people living our lives on planet earth and trying to milk acceptance out of people and the world. God was moved by His great love to do something to solve our dilemma, to make it possible for us to undergo a radical change in nature. He gives us the opportunity to get a heart transplant. ("I will remove the heart of stone [hard] and give you a heart of flesh [pliable]" [Ezek. 36:26]). With this new heart, we can begin to look to Him to supply all our needs, which is as it should be.

God solved your problem in the lovely Jesus. Every answer to our dilemma is wrapped up in Him. It's imperative, however, that we understand *how* Jesus is the solution to the problem if we're to be able to appropriate Him as our answer.

In this chapter, we will consider phase one of God's redemptive solution, the reason you and I needed redeeming. I urge you to read it in detail, even if you feel you already have a thorough understanding of the Fall.

Realizing that some of you may like a more detailed explanation of a tenet as I do, I have created several appendixes for this purpose. The ideas developed in each appendix are referenced in the text which follows.

Model of Man

Let's start by developing a simple Biblical model of man. The Lord used Charles Solomon and his book *Handbook to Happiness* (Tyndale) to help me in this area, and I'm very grateful for his insights. I have taken the basic idea and modified it.

We cannot take the most complicated being God ever created and adequately represent him with a two-dimensional diagram. But our understanding of the Word of God can be greatly helped if we employ diagraming as a communication vehicle.

Each individual is, of course, a whole, but the Word teaches that the whole person is composed of three integrated parts: spirit, soul, and body (Figure 4.1, also see e.g., 1 Thess. 5:23).

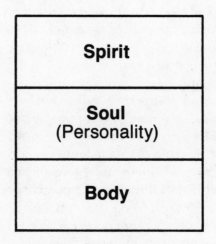

Figure 4.1

The Personality

Ask the typical Christian what his soul is and he'll be hard pressed to respond. "I don't know. It's like a puff of smoke or something," he might say. The word *soul* and the word *psychology* come from the same root, meaning "personality." The soul, then, is your personality—mind, will, and emotions—your unique version of them.

An Earthsuit, Not a Jupitersuit

Your body is the vehicle here on planet earth that houses your soul and spirit. Second Corinthians 5:1-8 refers to it as an earthly tent. Author C. S. Lovett has called it an "earthsuit," which seems a good way to describe it. It really is an earthsuit. God never designed it to live in Jupiter's environment. You might be able to take it there, but you'd have to encase it in an "earthy" environment or it would die.

The earthsuit is simply a vehicle through which my soul interacts with the earthly environment. As I write this, my soul is commanding the muscles in my earthsuit to make its fingers hit certain keys on a typewriter, and the earthsuit is trying its best to obey. You are commanding your earthsuit to make its eyes rove methodically across these rows of print, and as a result, my soul is communicating with yours. If we were face to face, we could command our lips to wiggle on our earthsuits and make noises cross over from one to another, which we'd then process and interpret. Again, we'd be using our earthsuits to communicate.

If my earthsuit should happen to fall over and die while we were talking, you might phone the police and tell them you had just seen a man die. That would be the human view, but not God's. This man wouldn't have died. My earthsuit would have died. I'd still be alive and well and wingin' with Jesus.

The earthsuit is good. It's not an evil thing, but it's vulnerable to being used by the devil to get or keep us in a lot of trouble. There are some very neat things to be experienced on planet earth through the earthsuit. It feels good to feed it Mexican food when it's hungry. It feels good to give it a hot shower when its muscles are tired. It feels good to sex it when it's sexy. All these are *good* things. God made the earthsuit and designed it to enjoy these things, but they must be done according to the manufacturer's handbook or we're creating trouble for ourselves.

God Doesn't Have an Earthsuit

The Scriptures also teach that God is spirit and that humanity is made in His image. Therefore, we are spirit-beings. *We are not physical creatures with spirits; we are spirit-creatures with bodies.* God doesn't have an earthsuit. He doesn't need one. He's using ours if we're born again. He lives in here with me! However, for a few years He used an earthsuit that was exclusively His own. He called Himself "Jesus, Son of God." Jesus *is* God. The Scriptures state, "God was in Christ reconciling the world to Himself" (2 Cor. 5:19); "He is the image of the invisible God" (Col. 1:15); "He who has seen Me [Jesus] has seen the Father" (John 14:9).

While He was walking here on earth, Jesus made it clear that there was a way for us to get our problem solved with God the Father. He said first that a person has to be born a second time, literally "born from above" according to John 3. Nicodemus said, "You mean I've got to get back inside my mom?"

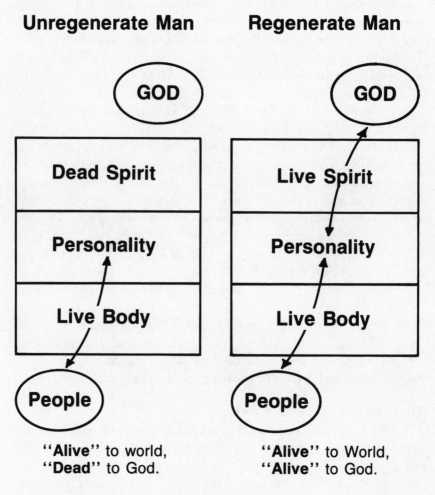

Unregenerate Man

Regenerate Man

GOD

GOD

Dead Spirit

Live Spirit

Personality

Personality

Live Body

Live Body

People

People

"**Alive**" to world,
"**Dead**" to God.

"**Alive**" to World,
"**Alive**" to God.

Figure 4.2

"No, Nick, you've got it all wrong," Jesus said. "That would give you two earthsuits, and you don't need two. One to the customer is adequate. But you don't have a spirit-vehicle. Your spirit is dead. You've got to get a live spirit, and then you can commune with My Father through that vehicle." ("Those who worship Him must worship in spirit" [John 4:24]).

By being born from above through receiving Christ as Savior, a redeemed person acquires a second vehicle through which he can express himself in addition to his earthsuit. He can now fellowship with people through his earthsuit and with God through his spirit.

The unsaved person has a live earthsuit through which he relates to others, but a dead spirit. The Bible says he is "dead in his sins" (see Eph. 2:1-10) and thus is not alive to God now, nor will he be so in eternity unless he appropriates Christ's provision by choosing to get spiritually born from above. Figure 4.2 illustrates this.

The Brain Is a Computer

Working with that overall model of man, let's now break the soul down into its three component parts: mind, will, and emotions—your thinker, your chooser, and your feeler. Then let's add a brain to our model. The brain *must* be a part of the body (see Figure 4.3). Logic will dictate that the brain and the mind

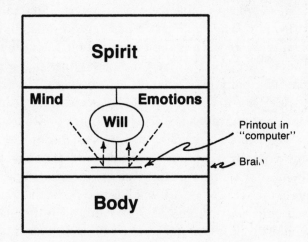

Figure 4.3

cannot be the same, because the brain is made out of meat. It's going to stay right here on earth when your earthsuit dies. If, therefore, your mind were your brain, your mind would stay here in your dead body. That would leave you nothing to think with after physical death, and that's not the picture the Bible gives us (see e.g., Luke 16:23-31). Thus, your mind cannot be your brain. Your mind *uses* your brain here on earth, but the brain is simply a hunk of meat like a heart or a liver.

The brain does have a unique function, however: it's a computer. The reason they call a computer a mechanical brain is that they got their inspiration for designing one by analyzing the way a human brain works. The brain is simply a data processing unit. It gathers information from the environment through the body's sensory preceptors (eyes, ears, etc.) and organizes these data into structures we call "meaning." "Printouts" would be the computer term.

Your brain generates 5,000 printouts per hour, I suppose, and it couldn't care less what it processes. You let your eyes scan the covers of the sex magazines, and you'll get printouts of naked women every time. Focus your ears on listening to the Word of God being taught in a church, and you'll get printouts of that. Garbage in, garbage out; truth in, truth out. Your brain will process whatever is fed into it.

When you have a computer in operation, you must have some people available called computer analysts if you're to benefit from it. Their job is to read the printouts, analyze them, and then make recommendations to the big boss. He then makes decisions based on their recommendations. As his decisions go, so goes company production (performance).

God has made human beings in a similar fashion. Your mind and your emotions are your computer analysts. They sort of sit in there and watch TV all day. As the printouts come flying through your computer, mind and emotions rapidly analyze them, react, then quickly make recommendations to the big boss, the will. Now, the will has two polarities like a light switch; you either *do* or you *don't*. You can't sit in the middle, since that would be choosing not to choose, and that's a don't.

You either do or you don't.

Will Is the Big Boss

Christians have a free will that can override the recommendations of both mind and emotions. The mind could say to the will, "I don't understand why the Lord is letting this happen to me," and the will can answer, "Well, rain on whether I understand or not; I choose to believe it'll all work to my ultimate good, because the Word says so."

The emotions could say, "I feel excited about the prospect of asking my secretary out to lunch today." And the will can say, "Oh, no you don't, Tiger! I choose to do the will of my Father!"

You see, Christian, we're really on the hook to obey God. We now have a free will that can rule over and resist the "recommendations" of our emotions. The trick is to understand *how*, which we'll explain in great detail in later chapters.

Long after I had become a new creation in Christ, I made a startling discovery. I had always thought that eternal life was an extension or a continuation of *my life*. My life began in 1927, and I assumed that when I accepted Christ as my personal Savior, God attached an extension onto my life that would last forever. That's not true. Why would God want to take the Lord-of-the-Ring life that had separated me from His presence in the first place and extend it forever? His plan was to exterminate my old life and exchange it for new life. And that life is a person, Jesus Christ.

"What was from the beginning, what we have heard, what we have seen with our eyes, what we beheld and our hands handled, concerning the Word of Life — and *the* life was manifested, and we have seen and bear witness and proclaim to you *the* eternal life . . ." (1 John 1:1, 2, emphasis added). John claims he actually *handled* and *saw* eternal life! Eternal life is not an "it." Eternal life is Jesus! Thus, a critical part of victorious living is comprehending *how* to let eternal life (Christ) be expressed through my personhood to do His will (see Appendix A).

In my workshop I have a drill, a saw, and a grinder. All three serve different functions, yet all three are plugged into the same power source, the electric outlet. The electricity is their "life." The "life" doesn't make them all identical. It actually *gives them their unique identity*. So long as the "life" flows, each of these tools *manifests its true identity*. It's the life that reveals their uniqueness and purpose for being. Without that life they all become paperweights.

Time Out

Eternal life (Christ) is not time dimensional. "All things came into being by Him; and apart from Him nothing came into being that has come into being" (John 1:3). Christ created *all* things. Therefore, there is no such thing as a "natural phenomenon." If it exists in its natural state, He created it. This includes the time dimension; time was created by the Lord. Therefore, logically, He is not time dimensional. If He were, the created would be superior to the Creator. Thus, Christ is not time dimensional. He is *supratime*. And the time dimension as we see it in our finite existence is actually present tense in His perception.

Let's suppose your earthwalk were represented by the Main Street of an old western movie set. Every episode in your life is represented by a store front on the street (see Figure 4.4).

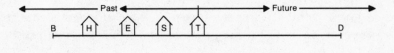

Figure 4.4

The letter "B" stands for your physical birth, the "H" represents your first haircut, the "E" is your entry into elementary school, the "S" is the day you invited Jesus Christ to become your Savior and Lord, the "T" stands for today, and the "D" is for physical death. To you, the portion from T to the left represents the past, T represents the present, and everything to the right of T stands for the future. This is because you are a time-bound creature.

God is, however, like a person who is hovering over your Main Street in a helicopter. Since He is not time dimensional, He can see the whole street all at once (see Figure 4.5).

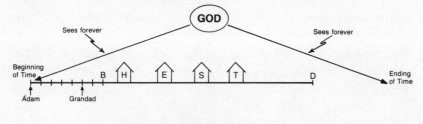

Figure 4.5

God is all-knowing (omniscient); that's one of His attributes. This doesn't make us robots who are not free to make choices. Quite the contrary, you are a free moral agent who may make fifty choices before you finish reading this chapter. But God, being all-knowing, sees the fifty buildings representing your choices as present-tense reality. Read Psalm 139. It says He knows your thoughts before you ever generate them! Now, I can't figure this out completely; no one can. I just have to accept the Word of God, which says His ways are higher than mine. And time is a meaningless concept to His perception, where everything is present tense.

Since God is not time dimensional, He can see forever into the future. That's how He dictated the Revelation to John. But consider also that He can see forever into the past as well. If He couldn't, He'd be limited by time just as we are.

The Bible states that Jesus Christ is "the Lamb slain from the foundation of the world" (Rev. 13:8, KJV). Imagine this now! God solved the "problem" before the problem ever occurred in the time dimensional setting by "seeing" the lovely, innocent Jesus crucified before the foundation of the world.

Snakebitten!

Now let's bring Adam, the first man, into the picture. He produced a bunch of descendants, one of which was you. But what would have happened to you if your grandfather had died before he ever got his wife pregnant (see Figure 4.5)? You would have died in his gene pool and never shown up on planet earth. That obviously didn't happen, but Romans 5:12 says that in some manner it *did* happen to you in Adam. Somehow, when that first man died, all men died. How? What part of me died before I ever showed up? Let's return to that garden scene. You, too, were there, in Adam's loins (see Figure 4.6).

Thinking in terms of our model-of-man diagram again, the Lord and Adam fellowshipped with one another regularly because Adam was created with an innocent spirit that made him alive to God.

One day God said to him, "Adam, you may do anything in this garden you wish except one thing. You may not eat from the 'no-no' tree." Now, there had to be a no-no of some sort or Adam would have been a robot who had no choice to rebel against God's authority over him. God further said, "The *very day* you eat from that tree, you will die." Notice, He didn't say Adam would die hundreds of years later. He said he would die by sundown.

Adam and God fellowship through Adam's innocent spirit.

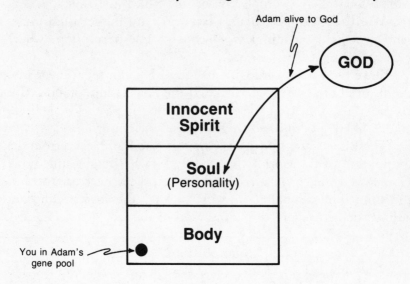

Figure 4.6

God was not implying a physical death by the end of the day. Had that been the case, we would have died physically at sundown in Adam, and none of the rest of us would have ever been born. Well then, did Adam and Eve die soulically? Did their personalities die? No, in that case they would have become robots who could not think, feel, or choose. In this condition, they would have produced "after their kind," and we'd all be robots today.

We've ruled out all but one part of man, his spirit. Their spirits died! That part of Adam and Eve that made them alive to God died, and after sundown they could no longer fellowship with Him (see Figure 4.7). They then began to produce spiritually dead offspring whose normal, natural state was to be dead to God and, by nature, to rebel against His authority over them, claiming their "right to live their own lives." They became the first Lords of the Ring.

Sin

The Scriptures say in Romans 5:12 that simultaneous with man's first act of rebellion against God's right to authority over him, something entered into the world called "sin." On the basis of its subsequent use in much of Romans 5–8, this cannot always have reference to just one sinful act, but rather to a power called sin entering into man's experience. I do not claim to understand exactly what this is other than to say what the Word says. It is an "evil . . . *present* in me" (Rom. 7:21, emphasis added), a "*different* law in . . . my *body*" (Rom. 7:23, emphasis added). Terms such as "the power of sin," "the law of sin," "the principle of sin," or simply "sin" are synonyms. A quick scan over Romans 7 will demonstrate that "sin" often refers to an evil power against which the Christian battles. We will describe this battle in detail later.

When Adam sinned against God's authority, not only did his innocent spirit die to God so that he had no life toward God, but *his spirit instantly became one with Satan*. Adam's dead spirit was instantly unified with Satan's spirit, the power of sin. This power of sin entered into Adam and took control over him spirit, soul, and body. He became Satan's spirit-offspring, born of the same rebellion as he, a dead spirit being in human form totally submissive to Satan (see Eph. 2:1, 2).

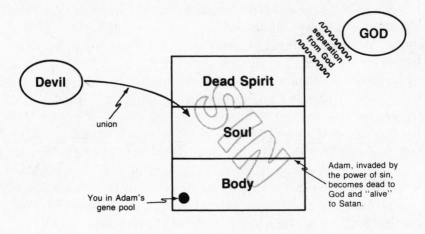

Figure 4.7

What a Difference You've Made in My Life!

Let's briefly examine the disastrous change that took place in Adam's life as a result of his having overthrown God's theocracy on earth. Not only was his spirit now dead, but his soul and body were now dying by degrees as well. If he didn't repent before he ejected from his dying earthsuit, he'd have to exist forever as a dead spirit-son of Satan in hell.

Mind

The Word describes a lost person as having a darkened mind, as having a veil over his mind (see e.g., Eph. 4:17, 18). This means that he cannot understand the things of God. He has no spiritual comprehension. The Bible will be meaningless to him in terms of being able to discern spiritual enlightenment from it. He may earn a Ph.D. in Bible but still not know anything about spiritual truth.

Will

The lost person also has a rebellious will. He will not, indeed he cannot, submit to God's authority over him. He chafes at God's ways, seeing them as burdensome. He sees God as an authoritarian party pooper. His theme song is "I Did It My Way."

He fits perfectly into the "Me Generation" of the world today. He is his own god. He insists on ruling over his own personal kingdom.

Emotions

The emotions of a person like Adam are for worldly affection. He loves the world, the system of the world, the way it's structured. He lives to satisfy his needs. He lives to feel good. He enjoys life separated from God. He'd like to be age twenty-one on earth forever.

Body

Adam's body was dying. It was headed for the dirt. It was just a matter of time before its warranty ran out.

This is what Adam became with the Fall. His offspring now abound.

The Sin Nature

Just what is the sin nature, anyway? First, it is not a Biblical term in that it does not appear in the original Greek text of the New Testament, even though some translations such as the *New International Version* employ it. No doubt theologians have generated this term to describe a condition in man. It describes any person who is *dead to God*, any person with a dead spirit. Synonyms are "old nature," "Adamic nature," "old man," "old self," "unregenerate nature," "lower nature," "natural man," "sinner," and "in Adam."

The word *sin* has several definitions, one of which is "rebellion against God." The word *nature* means the "natural characteristics" of anything. Birds have a flying nature. It is a hog's nature to wallow in the mud. No one need teach him to do this; it is instinctive to him. Thus, the term "sin nature" simply means a natural bent to rebel against God's authority, to view God as a party pooper, unnecessary in one's life, someone I can live quite well without, someone to whom I refuse to submit. In short, I refuse to acknowledge Him as *my* God. *I* am my god. I do things *my* way. I am Lord of My Ring.

Thus, for example, since I have a sex drive that I enjoy satisfying, *I* will decide the best way to satisfy it. I reject God's plan as too limited. I will feast from the sexual smorgasbord, sating myself, my way.

Note a very important fact, however. We must not observe a person's behavior and, from that point of reference, infer his nature. It isn't the flying that makes a bird a bird; it's his *birth* that makes a bird a bird. Similarly, it's not a man's adulterous behavior that identifies him as having a dead spirit. We must use the Word of God to make that determination, and the Bible will make such a determination on the basis of the man's *birth*, not his performance. If he is still a spirit-son of Satan in Adam's lineage by his first birth, he has a dead spirit. If he has become a spirit-son of God by a second, spiritual birth in the second Adam, Jesus, he has a live spirit. In either case, it is his birth, not his performance, that determines his identity according to the Bible (see e.g., Eph. 2:4-6).

There you have a brief description of our basic makeup and our fatal problem with sin just because we're part of the human race. Next we'll consider how God provided a way out of the dilemma.

Questions for Further Study

1. As a descendant of Adam, what significance did his spiritual death have for you?

2. What determines your basic nature?

3. What is your understanding of Christ as your life? Does this make you a hollow tube (i.e., no personality and individuality) that Jesus flows through?

4. Give your understanding of whether your bodily desires are sinful.

FIVE

A "NEW MAN" IN AN OLD EARTHSUIT

One of actor Jimmy Stewart's most famous films is titled "It's a Wonderful Life." In that picture, Stewart plays a despairing young banker who thinks he'd be better off dead. And through the rest of the movie, an angel shows him what the world would be like if he did indeed leave the scene.

In a sense, the lives of most people are like that of the Jimmy Stewart character. While they're living and breathing physically, a vital part of them — the spirit — is dead. It was dead on arrival when they entered this world because of the choice made by Adam.

Even if you're not a Christian you, too, were a spiritual stillbirth. You were born dead. You also inherited this condition from Adam. In this chapter, I'll use the Word to show that God solved your problem of being cut off from His acceptance by crucifying your Adamic identity in Christ and causing a brand-new spirit-you to be born in Christ's resurrection. Now, because of the finished work of Christ, God finds it delightfully easy to totally accept the new you (see Appendix B).

Christ in Me; I in Christ

Salvation is a two-sided coin. Side A represents Jesus' coming into the believer; side B represents the believer's coming into Jesus. He is in me, and I am in Him. This is a package deal; you can't get one side at a time.

The astounding thing is that for every verse you can find in the New Testament stating that the believer is indwelt by Christ, you will discover *ten* verses stating that the believer indwells Jesus. Ten to one! But until very recent years, I could count on one hand the number of messages I'd heard on what it means to be "in Christ."

I've heard thousands of sermons on the one side of the relationship, how to get Christ to come into you and save you. Praise the Lord for those messages! But on the other hand, if the Word is weighted ten to one with side B verses, do you see that many Christians are being fed on short rations? A straight diet of salvation messages to the Church won't bring us to maturity. God makes that clear to us in Hebrews 6:1: "Therefore *leaving* the elementary teaching about the Christ, let us press on to maturity, not laying *again* a foundation of repentance" (emphasis added).

John 3:16 served up in eighty-seven ways to the believer is not God's plan for victory. A Christian will starve on such a milk diet. That teaching won't help me much when I experience an assault on my self-esteem and feel rejected. I need power to resist; I don't need to quote John 3:16. I need to know how to appropriate what side B is all about.

Side B *(In Christ)*

Consider a few of the verses that speak of the believer's being in Christ, side B. What does the Bible state that God accomplished for you *in* Christ? How did this solve the problem of your alienation from Him? Consider Ephesians 1:4: "[God] chose us in Him before the foundation of the world." In some way, God placed you into the lovely, innocent Jesus before the world was formed. That doesn't mean you had no choice, but God saw the

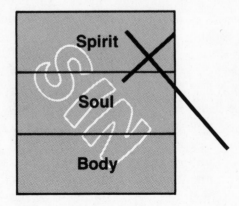

Figure 5.1

problem before time ever began (see Appendix C). He saw your need before you even had one!

Thus, imagine yourself being in Christ as He came to planet earth to solve your problem. God placed you *in* Him. Ultimately, He went to the Cross. Where were you? In Him. As the lovely, innocent Jesus died, you, too, were crucified. The difference is that you deserved it and He didn't. But it wasn't your earthsuit that died; not the physical you, but the *spiritual* you (see Figure 5.1).

That rebel you, that Lord-of-the-Ring you, that spiritually dead you, that spirit-son of Satan was crucified with Him. "I *have been* crucified with Christ," Paul said (Gal. 2:20, emphasis added). "Knowing this, that our old self was crucified with Him" (Rom. 6:6). Romans 6 and 7 and many other verses in the Word of God state categorically that all believers *died* when Christ died. The verbs in the Greek are all *past* tense. You and I *were* executed *in* Christ (side B). *God executed everything about you He could not tolerate in His holy presence* and buried you with Jesus (see Rom. 6:4; Col. 2:12). That's what water baptism is all about. It's a pantomime of your co-death and rebirth in Christ.

Dear Christian, the Word unequivocally states in each of the verses cited above that when Christ died, you died. You *must* deal with those verses. You must deal with the question, "*What* died?" I have dealt with it, arrived at the conclusion that it was the old self, the old identity that died; and have appropriated this in my own life. When I did all that, I immediately began to experience a vastly more consistent victory over lifelong hang-ups.

If you say, "No, Bill, I know you mean well, but the old self did not actually die," then you must answer the question, "What *did* die?" You cannot be intellectually honest with yourself and God by simply sweeping under the rug this abundance of Scripture referring to your death in Christ. This truth permeates much of Paul's writings. You have to come to grips with that before the Lord. What died? It was everything about the former "you" that God could not tolerate in His holy presence. The old you, your old spiritual identity, was executed and replaced by a lovely, new, godly you. In Christ, at salvation, you were not only given a new present and a new future, you were given a new *past!* Your spiritual roots are no longer in Adam, but in Christ.

Christ's Blood for Your Sins
Christ's Body for Your Sin (Nature)

All born-again people know that God solved the problem with their sin*s* (performance) through the shed *blood* of Jesus Christ: "without the shedding of blood there is no forgiveness" (Heb. 9:22*b*). But what the vast majority of Christians have *not* seen is that God solved the problem *with the source*, your old man, through the *body* of Christ on the Cross. "We *have been sanctified* through the offering of the *body* of Jesus Christ once for all" (Heb. 10:10, emphasis added). That goes even beyond forgiveness. It means that as new creatures *in* Christ, we have been made pure and holy before God through the body of Christ, not through His blood.

The blood and the body of Christ are both critically important. Did you ever stop to ask yourself why we partake of *two* elements at the Lord's Supper since it is the blood of Jesus that has cleansed us from our sins? Why did Jesus introduce the wine *and* the bread? Why not just the wine since it is to remind us of our forgiveness bought with His precious blood? Forgiveness is all that is ever mentioned in most churches as we partake of the elements. But that's only observing half the celebration.

The bread, the second element, represents Christ's *body* in which God crucified our old son-of-Satan, self-centered, sin nature—the old man. The bread is to remind us to commemorate the execution of our old identity through our co-death in His body, in which that old rebel who refused to submit to God's rightful authority, who insisted on playing Lord of the Ring, was eliminated and replaced by a brand new person in Christ who *desires* to do God's will. "Therefore if any man is in Christ, he *is* a new creature; the old things *passed* away; behold, new things *have* come" (2 Cor. 5:17, emphasis added). This new person really desires to submit to God's authority and desires his life to be lived to bring glory to the Lord Jesus. That's a ten!

No Siamese Twins

Please understand that God had no plan for joining His Holy Spirit to any person's old sin nature. He had no plan to give birth to spiritual Siamese twins who are half spirit-child of Satan through Adam and half spirit-child of God through

Christ. Jesus said, "Any city or house divided against itself shall not stand" (Matt. 12:25). God would never set you up for guaranteed failure by making you a "house divided against yourself." I'll agree that my experience and my feelings at times "tell" me I am a house divided, but since God would never set me up for certain failure, I must search His Word to find another cause for my strife within. I am not a house divided.

Jesus made this very clear, and the body of Scripture documents it. He said you couldn't sew a patch of new cloth on an old garment. He meant this as an analogy of the new man and the old man. It's futile to try to join them together, and God did not make a lie of Jesus' teaching. Jesus said you can't put *new* wine (the Holy Spirit) into *old* skins (the old nature), because the old skins can't contain the glory of His presence. You've got to put the new wine into *new* skins (new nature).

The Scriptures likewise say you cannot join light (Holy Spirit) with darkness (old man). The Word further says that a believer (live-spirit child of God) must never join himself in marriage to an unbeliever (dead-spirit child of Satan). We know He would never violate His own admonition by joining into union the old man and the new man inside your earthsuit.

Jesus said, "No one can serve two masters" (Matt. 6:24). Now I ask you, would God who taught all the foregoing truths deliberately "set up" the Christian by giving him two conflicting identities, one loyal to God, the other equally loyal to Satan? No! Lost people have *one* master (Satan), not two. Christians also have *one* master (God), not two. But your *former* master constantly tempts and badgers you to submit to him again.

My True Identity in Christ

Let's take a Biblical look at the sort of "raw material" this new spirit man is made of whom God has created to live with Him forever. What sort of *nature* does he have? To do this, we must not speculate, but examine the verses which speak of our being "in Christ," "in Him," "in whom," etc. We must note the verb tenses to determine whether they speak of some future nature we shall acquire or if they speak of present day reality. This will then reveal your true identity.

- You are justified and redeemed (already). (Rom. 3:24)
- Your old self was killed (crucified). (Rom. 6:6)
- You are not condemned. (My performance is condemned when I don't trust in His life through me, but God does not condemn the *performer*, just the *performance*.) (Rom. 8:1)
- You are free from the law of sin and death. (Rom. 8:2)
- You are accepted. (All my life I've sought to be accepted. Now I am!) (Rom. 15:7)
- You are sanctified (holy, set apart). (1 Cor. 1:2)
- You have wisdom, righteousness, sanctification, redemption (I am ransomed — restored to favor). (1 Cor. 1:30)
- You are *always* led in His triumph (whether it appears so or not). (2 Cor. 2:14)
- Your hardened mind has been removed. (2 Cor. 3:14)
- You are a new creature. (Even though I don't always feel or act like it, my deep desire is to do so.) (2 Cor. 5:17)
- You are the righteousness of God. (You can't get more righteous than this.) (2 Cor. 5:21)
- You are liberated. (Gal. 2:4)
- You are joined with all believers (not inferior to anyone). (Gal. 3:28)
- You are a son and an heir. (Gal. 4:7)
- You are blessed with every spiritual blessing in heaven. (Eph. 1:3)
- You are chosen, holy, and blameless before God. (Eph. 1:4)
- You are redeemed, forgiven. (Eph. 1:7)
- You *have* obtained an inheritance. (Eph. 1:10, 11)
- You are sealed with the Spirit. (Eph. 1:13)
- You are alive (formerly a dead spirit). (Eph. 2:5)
- You are seated in heaven (already). (Eph. 2:6)
- You are created for good performance. (And I can let Christ live through me to perform it.) (Eph. 2:10)
- You have been brought near to God. (Eph. 2:13)
- You are a partaker of the promise. (Eph. 3:6)
- You have boldness and confident access to God (not slinking as a "whipped dog"). (Eph. 3:12)
- You were *formerly* darkness, but are *now* light. (Eph. 5:8)
- You are a member of His body (not inferior to other members). (Eph. 5:30)

- Your heart and mind are guarded by the peace of God. (Peace is *knowing* something, not always *feeling* it.) (Phil. 4:7)
- You have all your needs (not greeds) supplied. (Phil. 4:19)
- You are complete (perfect). (Col. 2:10)
- You are raised up with Him. (Col. 3:1)
- Your life is hidden with Christ in God. (Col. 3:3)

This is who God raised up in Christ. You are not grubby. You are glorious in your nature! The *new natural you* is really someone special. You are a child of God as Jesus said in John 1:12, and as the Word repeats in many verses such as Galatians 3:26: "For you are all sons of God through faith in Christ Jesus." And *He* is now your life. He will live the same life through you that He lived through His own earthsuit when He walked the planet if you will cooperate with Him. This means a supernatural life of agape, *not a life of constantly striving to get your needs met.* Jesus Christ wants to express through you what the Father expressed through Him, bringing love and hope to a hurting world, beginning with your own house.

Sinner Saved by Grace or Saint Who Sins?

Earlier, I made the point that it is birth, not performance, that dictates nature. Humanity's definition of a sinner is performance-based. If a person sins, he's a sinner. But that is not God's definition. His view is that a sinner is a sinner because he was born that way, and neither good nor bad performance can alter it. It's not sins that send a person to hell; his *nature* sends him to hell. All you have to do to go to hell is be born and get old enough to be accountable. Unless you submit to God's plan to get your nature changed, you're sunk!

When a sinner gets saved, he does not become a sinner saved by grace. He becomes a saint who sins. The way the worldly man sees it, a saint is a person who rarely sins. We usually reserve this label for people who are too old to sin! We refer to them as "dear old saints," but we never speak of "dear young saints." The label is bestowed as a reward for years of good performance. If we teach a Sunday school class for forty years or serve as a church officer for thirty, we may have a chance to be referred to as a "saint" in our golden years. That's not God's

Word, however; it's human religious tradition.

Fifty-six times *after* the Cross, the Word refers to born-again people as "saints" (mostly penned by Paul), whereas it uses the term *sinner* rarely when referring to a Christian. One definite reference, however, is where Paul proclaims that he is chief of sinners in 1 Timothy 1:15. How can we deal with this apparent contradiction?

My friend Lee LeFebre uses a helpful analogy to explain Paul's intent. Suppose you were a high jumper in college and you broke the school record by a foot. The school placed a mark on the gym wall with your name beside it, showing the height of your jump and proclaiming you champion, or "chief." Twenty years later you walk into the gym. There is your mark on the wall. No one has even come close to breaking your record. You're still the chief. This is what Paul meant.

Saul of Tarsus was the number one performer of all time who ever tried to earn his way into God's acceptance. According to God's Word that makes him the most "mature," the "gold medal winner," the "highest" or the "chiefest" of sinners.

Whether you accept that explanation or not, however, the fact remains that the Word gives us a fifty-six to three ratio of "saint" over "sinner." Traditional teaching clings to the two or three because of the erroneous, performance-based definition of saint and sinner. By faith, through understanding the new creation in Christ, I'm accepting the fifty-six.

Whose Life Arose Out of the Tomb

Did your old sin nature have resurrection power? Could that life walk out of a grave? No. It had no such capability. Was God interested in resurrecting *that* life? If so, then why co-crucify you in the first place? That would be meaningless and futile. Only one life has victory over death.

Tell me, will you obtain that life some day, or have you already got it (Him)? If you are born anew, you *already have* eternal life in the person of *Jesus*. Eternal life is a synonym for Jesus (see 1 John 1:1, 2). So now that you are new in Christ, how does the Word of God describe your *present* life? It states that Christ *is* your life. Colossians 3:3, 4a says, "For you *have died* and your life is hidden with Christ in God. When Christ, who *is* our life . . ."

(emphasis added). Did that say you died? Yes! When did you die? You died in Christ's body when He died. How did you get alive again? You were made new *in* Him, and He is now *your* life.

Because these things are true, God's plan is that you would cooperate with Christ to let Him express His life by filtering that life through your personality and earthsuit. Do you think *He* could hack it in your circumstances? I wonder if His life would be able to "bypass" all those old, green highways in your brain and work directly through your new spirit to empower your personality, using your body for good to minister to a hurting world?

Dear Christian, the Lord never intended you to try your best to live the Christian life. He placed His Spirit *within* you to live His life through you to bring glory and honor to Himself. *He* does His work of ministry on earth through you. The battle is the Lord's.

Your new purpose is different from your old one of seeking to get all your needs supplied by using the old ways you learned beginning early in life. Your new purpose is to glorify Jesus. God has given you a *new* heart and has written *His* desires upon your heart and mind (Heb. 10:14-16).

God has also placed His own Spirit within you to enable you to live out the law of love prophesied in Ezekiel 36:26, 27: "Moreover, I will give you a new heart and put a new spirit within you; and I will remove the heart of stone from your flesh and give you a heart of flesh. And I will put My Spirit within you and cause you to walk in My statutes, and you will be careful to observe My ordinances." Yes, this prophecy was given to the Israelites, but it is *present-day reality* in all believers. You and I are already the *spirit*-children of Abraham. Jews are the *physical* children and their time for the fulfillment of that prophecy is yet future.

The Airborne Infantry

No, I am not going to discuss the rapture. I'm going to speak of something that has already happened, another basic truth about the Christian life. Jesus remained on earth forty days after the resurrection, and then He ascended to the right hand of the

Father. Now, if you are *in* Him, where are you right now? Ephesians 2:5, 6 says, "Even when we *were* dead in our transgressions [He] made us alive together with Christ . . . and *raised* us [already] up with Him, and *seated* us [already] with Him in the heavenly places, *in* Christ Jesus [side B]" (emphasis added). This is all *spiritual*, not physical (see Figure 5.2).

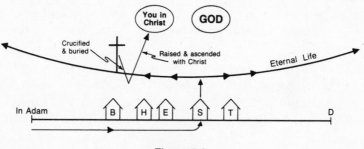

Figure 5.2

In other words, *we are already there, friend.* You say, "I don't *feel* like I'm in heaven." Well, never mind how you *feel*. God says you *are* there, and if your feeler seems to tell you that you aren't, which is the liar, God or your feeler? Read Colossians 3:1-4, paying special attention to the verb tenses, and see where God states you are right *now*:

> If then you *have been raised* up with Christ, keep seeking the things above, where Christ is, seated at the right hand of God. Set your mind on the things above, not on the things that are on earth. For you *have died* and your life *is* hidden with Christ in God. When Christ, who *is our life*, is revealed, then you also will be revealed with Him in glory. (emphasis added)

We *are* in heaven, but we must accept and appropriate this as factual on the basis of God's statement, not by what our five senses tell us is true.

The old "rebel you" was crucified in Christ and buried. The "new you" was born, raised, and ascended into heaven where you are in Christ, totally accepted and loved.

Clue to Why We Still Sin

God's plan was to execute the rebellious man and give birth to a new spirit-creation, one who adores Him and has His law of love written on his heart and mind. *But He placed this new man into the same old earthsuit. It has the same old brain with the same old, green highways in it.* Oh, oh! That's going to cause a problem, because it's going to be through those old, green highways that the Evil One will try to control the new man and get him to dance to the *old* tune (see Figure 5.3).

The new man is born in Christ's resurrection from the grave. The power of sin is now limited to the body. Flesh is a function of the brain.

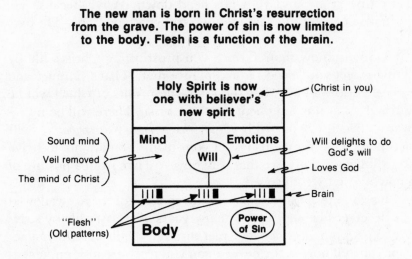

Figure 5.3

Someone says, "Oh, no, Bill, you don't understand. That's just the way God sees us. It's positional truth." Listen to me: *there is no such thing as "positional truth."* The Bible speaks only of truth and deception. The term *positional truth* is simply Satan's deception that will block you from accepting the present reality of God's solution to your problem. He has now accepted the new you, and He finds it delightfully easy to do so. Ask the Holy Spirit right now to reveal to you your true identity as you study just a very few of the abundance of verses in this chapter that document the identity of any person who is *in* Christ rather than *in* Adam.

Are You Experiencing Christ's Life Through You?

What are you doing with His life during your earthwalk? Are you still running around trying to milk acceptance and self-esteem out of the world like lost people when you've already *got* *both*? Are you still employing the same old methods, such as trying to perform for others to get them to accept you, or striving to perform up to your flesh's standards to generate and maintain self-esteem moment by moment? You *are* of infinite worth. You *are* accepted. Not by people, perhaps, but by God! If you're rejected by certain people, welcome to the club. So was Jesus. But He didn't go around with His head down. Why? Because He *knew* it's not a feeling that matters; it's what you know. He *knew* He was accepted.

Do you know that? Or are you prostituting Christ's life by living to get your need for acceptance met? That's sinning, and you are still walking after the flesh, the results of which will be burned up at the Judgment Seat of Christ. There will be no reward, because you will *already have had your reward.* Self-acceptance. A "righteousness of your own." You are not to strive to *get* love; we don't live that way now. We live from a posture of knowing that we *are* loved.

It's time to go to the Lord and repent. You have swallowed the deceiver's lie and wasted many years of Christ's life by striving to get your need for love met through the flesh. You can accept yourself now as the new person you truly are in Him, just as the Father accepts you — perfectly.

Spend some time praising Him for His fantastic, gracious plan whereby He has solved the problem in sweet Jesus. Praise Him, dear relative! Go ahead and weep for joy! It will tickle Him to death. He'll weep for joy with you and hug your neck unabashedly, just as He did when the Prodigal Son came down the road to his father's home. You are totally accepted forever as the new creation you already are.

Questions for Further Study

1. What's the importance of grasping the side B truths (Christians are "in Christ") of salvation?

2. What was it within you that died when Christ was crucified?

3. Does God intend for *you* to live the Christian life? What is His plan?

4. You already identified some of your unique flesh patterns. As you study the Scriptures, looking at the verses referring to your being *in Christ*, what biblical statements do you find that are direct answers or counterparts to your flesh?

SIX

YOU *CAN* KEEP A
GOOD MAN DOWN

A while back, I received the following letter:

> Dear Bill,
> I don't know where to begin. You don't know me, but I feel
> so desperate, and it seems I have been under the pile for so
> long. I am hoping you can help.
> A friend loaned me your tape about our being crucified in
> Christ and born again as new creations. I've listened to it over
> and over again, but it just doesn't work for me. I know you'll
> think I'm stupid, but honestly, I'm trying as hard as I can to
> claim what you teach. It just doesn't work for me.
> It seems like I see a glimmer of hope, but when I try to
> claim what you say, nothing different happens. I'm still the
> same old me! It all seems so hopeless. Can you help me?

Bless her heart. I can identify! This sweet lady is asking the
pleading question, "But how do I do this?" She had gotten just
enough teaching to give her a glimmer of hope, but her friend
had unwittingly left town without giving her the "how-to"
teaching tapes. Satan's goal is to entice the believer into employing his same old fleshly techniques to get his human needs
satisfied, or, in the case of the Yukky Flesh Christian, create a
sense of hopeless despair. In this chapter, we'll see how he de-
ceives you.

But How?

The lady's question points to exactly the same problem Paul
addressed in Romans 7:18*b*: ". . . but how to perform that
which is good I find not" (KJV). Many Christians say "Amen"

85

and camp right there, failing to see Paul's "Thanks be to God" shout of victory in verse 25.

To better understand what caused him to shout verse 25, let's trust the Holy Spirit to enlighten us by studying the passage leading up to it.

Look at Romans 7:15, the defeated Christian's verse. "For that which I am doing, I do not understand; for I am not practicing what I would like to do, but I am doing the very thing I hate." How many actors are there in that verse? One: "I." Now jump down to Romans 7:20: "But if *I* am doing the very thing *I* do not wish, *I* am no longer the one doing it, but *sin* which dwells in me" (is the "one" doing it; emphasis added). How many actors do you count in this verse? Two: "I" and something called "sin." Somehow, an entity or power called sin is the "one" who wishes me to do "the very thing I hate." Something that *indwells* me wants me to rebel against God.

Now, I'm not teaching "the devil made me do it." He can't *make* me do anything. What I'm saying is an entity called sin somehow *suggested* that I do it. When I bought into sin's idea, it became mine, and *I* did the very thing I do not wish. Clearly, there are two actors identified in verse 20, but only one in verse 15. And clearly Paul says in verse 20 that he did not *want* to commit this sin, but that somehow this other actor was able to entice him into doing it.

I do not understand exactly *what* this entity is that the Bible calls sin, but I have an opinion that I expressed in Chapter 4. I believe it is Satan's counterfeit of the *Holy* Spirit, "the spirit that is now working in the sons of disobedience" (Eph. 2:2). Sin rules the spirit, soul, and body of the unregenerate person, but sin only indwells the *body* of the new creature in Christ (see Rom. 7:23).

The Deceiver

Many years ago when I recognized the truth of the preceding paragraph, I said, "Lord, there are two actors in verse 20 and only one in verse 15, yet I know that the *power of sin* was in this man in verse 15, too. Sin entered the human race at the Fall. How did sin manage to go underground to keep from being identified in verse 15?" And over a period of several weeks of examining and meditating on God's Word, I believe the Holy Spirit showed me how the Evil One operates.

Names are important in Scripture. You will often get marvelous truth by studying them. Satan is called "deceiver," "tempter," and "accuser," among other things. What's a deceiver? A deceiver is someone who will make you believe something is true when it's a lie. Or he will make you believe something is not true when, in fact, it is. Magicians are deceivers. They make you think they cut a lady into two pieces, when in fact they do not. And what part of you do they seek to deceive? Your *mind*.

The Word says that Satan "disguises himself as an angel of light" (2 Cor. 11:14). What is "light" in the Word? Truth! He can come at you as "truth," as "revelation," as "insight into reality." But how? It's simple. *He gives you a thought in your mind and disguises it to seem as if it is* your *thought*. You say, "How could he do that?" By speaking to you with *first-person singular* pronouns.

When the power of sin speaks to your mind, it does not use the pronoun "you," but the pronoun "I." Instead of experiencing the communication "Why don't *you* go ahead and give her a piece of your mind!" it will be served up to your mind as, "Well! *I* have a good mind to tell her off! By George, *I'm* going to do it!" And you often wind up "doing the very thing you hate." You grab the idea and convert it into action. You sin! Yes, *you* did the evil thing, but the *genesis* of it, the *origin* was the power of sin, *not* your mind. Let's go to the diagram again to explain how this spiritual warfare transpires in you.

In Figure 6.1, the shaded portion represents everything earthy. The curved surface represents the curvature of the earth, and everything below the horizon belongs to earth. It is not necessarily evil, just earthy. It belongs to this earthly dimension. Your body in its present form is in this category. It will never get to go into the presence of God (without being transfigured). Your body isn't evil; the Holy Spirit lives in it. It's neither good nor evil, but neutral. It's sort of like an oak tree; it can be used for a pulpit or a totem pole.

Satan's kingdom is here on planet earth. After the Fall, he was given the right to wage war against God and His people. His goal is to destroy God's plans and to usurp His Kingdom

"The Power of Sin's Channel To The Christian's Mind"

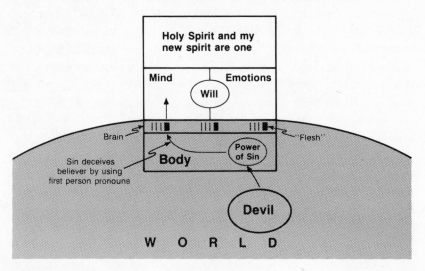

Figure 6.1

and His glory for himself. He's an egomaniac. Let's place him on earth in our diagram.

Satan has agents through which he works to accomplish his goals, including the world (system), the flesh, and (the power of) sin. Let's place the flesh and sin in their Biblical locations in our diagram. Employing our definition of "flesh" as "the old ways," we will place these green highways in the *brain*. These are the memory traces, the habit patterns, the software in your computer. If you are deceived into staying locked in on this software, your brain will play the same program over and over. The power of sin is located in the *body*, too. Romans 7:23 makes this location very clear: "I see a different law in the members of my body waging war against the law of my mind." Sin is in the body, *not* in the personality or the spirit. Your soul and spirit have been "sealed with the Spirit." They are holy now. My guess is that sin is located in the brain, but so as not to clutter the diagram, I will draw it elsewhere in the body.

God created you with needs. These are very good things. The idea is for you, the created, to turn to Him, the Creator, in total dependency on Him, worshiping Him, loving Him, fellow-shipping with Him, cooperating with Him and His plan for you. Part of this agreement is that He promises to "supply all your needs" (Phil. 4:19). But Satan's strategy is to get you to opt to live to get your needs met. He wants you to be deceived into making *this* your goal. Thus, he offers you "Plan B" for getting your needs supplied—your "old ways." That's what sin is all about. It is independence from God.

Macho Flesh

Let's take the sex drive, for example. It was God's idea to create it, not Satan's. Now, let's draw a curvy lady on our diagram (see Figure 6.2). You are parked in your car in front of the post office. Let's give you an eye on your earthsuit so you can see the lady walking by. The sunlight bounces off her earthsuit through your eye, up the optic nerve to your brain, where you get a printout of the curvy lady. Let's make you a male, a dedicated Christian, but let's give you an eight-lane, green highway for sexual lust. It's that wide line in your brain on the diagram.

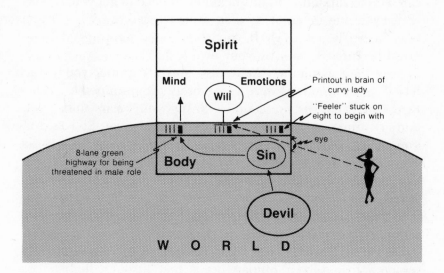

Figure 6.2

How did it get there? Oh, it could have resulted from many things, but let's say that your dad was strong as an acre of garlic. His strength, talent, and domination so intimidated you that you have spent many years struggling to measure up to his model, attempting to prove to your feeler that you are male. Your goal was to generate and maintain masculine self-esteem.

One of the ways you discovered to accomplish this along your journey as a god-player was to seduce women. It always made you feel so good about yourself when you could accomplish this. The chase and conquest were *so* satisfying. But you're saved now. Oh, yes! You are still *tempted* to seduce women to bolster your need to feel macho, but you don't *want* that. You long for victory over that. Your desire is different from your temptation. Your desire is good; your temptation is evil.

Let's add another variable to the mix. Let's say that your wife is the type of person who withholds sex from you if things are not all right on the home front. She has withheld herself from you for two weeks. Tell me, would this heighten your godly normal need for sexual satisfaction? Of course. The Bible says the spirit lusts against the flesh (see Gal. 5:17), so the word lust is not always an evil word. It simply means an accelerated appetite. Sin tries to capitalize on this heightened need to get you to rebel. "But each one is tempted when he is carried away . . . by his own lust" (James 1:14). If you receive the tempting thought, you'll be carried away by your own lusts.

But wait a minute. We've also got to consider your "stuck feeler." Your emotions were so intensely programmed by feeling threatened in your masculinity during your years under your dad's domination that they are stuck at level eight. So let's draw your stuck feeler as an eight-lane, green highway in the diagram. You feel the need to prove yourself male at level eight constantly. But to you this is normal, as you have long since renumbered your emotional Richter Scale and you call eight "one." The curvy lady is *not* the temptation. She's the *object* of the temptation. The *temptation is going to come from (the power of) sin*, Satan's agent through which he seeks to control. You are a saint being tempted to get your human needs met through fleshly techniques, acting like someone you are not (a sinner). You are not a sorry sinner just doing what comes naturally. *What you believe about your identity is what is going to make the difference. You will live out whatever you believe to be your true self, your true identity.*

Now, for the record, it's not a sin to be tempted. Jesus Himself "has been tempted in all things as we are, yet without sin" (Heb. 4:15). It is very normal for a Christian to be tempted. I have seen many Christians who spend a great deal of time begging God for forgiveness simply because they are *tempted* to do evil. That's error! Just being tempted doesn't make you guilty any more than it made Jesus guilty.

Sin simply waits until the printout of the curvy lady appears on the brain's visual screen (see Figure 6.2). Then as your mind considers this stimulus, sin, using the old, eight-lane, green highway in your brain, says to your mind, "Man, oh man, how *I'd* like to take her to bed." Wake up! Look at that pronoun, *I*. You see, it is actually the Evil One's agent sin, attempting to get you, a godly saint, to "do the very thing you hate." Notice that I have drawn a line from Satan through sin through the brain, traveling your flesh pattern for sexual lust and into the mind. You are being *presented* this idea for consideration. *You*, saint, *did not originate* this idea; he did. But if you buy it, you are sinning in your thought life. You will be totally guilty of sinning against God. You'll be acting like something you're *not*, a sinner. The Bible says we are now "partakers of the divine nature" (2 Pet. 1:4). As such, you do not want to rebel against God.

But let's say for illustration's sake that you do receive the thought from sin. When you buy into this thought, the rattle-snake illustration I used previously is activated. Feeler begins to respond to the stimulus of both curvy lady *and* sin's lustful thought. Remember, however, that you're not playing with a full deck in this battle. Your feeler is already sitting on an eight (or probably higher because of your wife's disobedience to the Lord's authority over her). So once your feeler starts to escalate, how long will it take it to get to ten? It'll hit ten before she passes the hood ornament on your car!

Now you've got sin hammering your mind with all sorts of creative ideas about how you can get your needs met, *and* you've got feeler slamming into will demanding satisfaction. "I *feel* I have to! I *feel* I can't refuse this! I *feel* I'm powerless!" Sit there and swallow this garbage for just a few, fleeting moments and you've lost the battle. You are playing with dynamite! Swallow the first thought and sin will follow that up with another: "*I* think *I'll* just get out and follow her into the post office. Man, what a walk!" Look at that pronoun again: *I*. It will seem as if the old man is alive and well. But if he is, God's Word is not true. Do you see it? The Evil One's strategy is to *disguise himself in your thought life as your old man* resurrected from the dead. But the old man has no resurrection capability. *He cannot resurrect. God* did not raise him up. Satan *can't* do it. But sin surely *can deceive* you by impersonating the old man in your thought life. And that is exactly how sin is controlling Christians.

Your victory lies in appropriating your true identity as the saint you are in Christ. You must counter the temptation along these lines: "No! I'm dead to that! That is not my thought. I recognize that strategy. It's true that I would like to get my sexual need satisfied, but my deep desire is to trust You to take care of that for me, Lord. That's Your problem, not mine." Then, *act* as though you're dead to sin's thoughts coming to you. How does a dead man respond when you try to stimulate him? He doesn't! He just sits there!

You, on the other hand, are alive! You are *dead* to the power of sin and *alive* to God in Christ Jesus. "Do not go on presenting the members of your body to [the power of] sin as instruments of righteousness; but present yourselves to God as those alive from

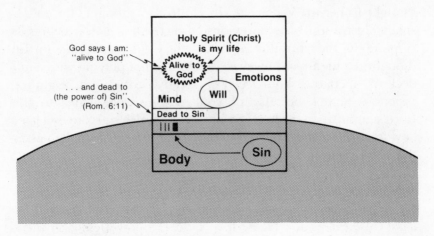

Figure 6.3

the dead, and your members as instruments of righteousness to God" (Rom. 6:13). Note in Figure 6.3 that I have placed the words "Dead to Sin" in the mind.

This is a faith (belief) position taken by the mind and will. God said that I am dead to sin but alive to God in Christ (see Rom. 6:11-13), so I will *choose* to *act* as if I'm dead to sin by *acting as though Christ is living through me* in this situation. I "set my mind" that Christ is expressing His life of victory over temptation through me, and I act as though it's true. I pray, "Well, Jesus, it sure is good to know that I am dead to this situation and You're living in it through me." And then I "flee from evil" (see 2 Tim. 2:22). "Gee, Lord, those are interesting bricks on the post office. I wonder how many there are under each window? Yes, there are seven. Isn't that interesting."

If the temptation occurred at some place like the checkout lane at the supermarket and it began to overwhelm me, I would simply *act* as if Jesus is living through me to say, "Excuse me, I've got to go get something else." And I'd act as though Christ through me is wheeling my cart out of the line to go to another lane. Friend, He will deliver you, but you must obey quickly. Stay there and sniff that good perfume of her's like a big Delbert Dumb and you're in deep trouble. Remember, you're playing with double dynamite due to your stuck feeler. Don't give your flesh even the smallest opening.

Hostile-Toward-Females Flesh

Now let's shift to another Christian who happens to be sitting in the car next to yours. This is a woman. She is a very committed, witnessing Christian leader. She, too, has her unique version of the flesh that she battles against. She has an eight-lane, green highway for hostility against females. Why would she have this sort of problem? Again, it could have resulted from various circumstances. In her case, she was rejected by her mom. Her mother was a Victorian sort of woman, very cold toward her daughter. When the child attempted to get involved in the cooking or baking, her mom would typically respond by telling her that things would go much faster and more efficiently if she would just leave the kitchen. "Get out of here. You're in my way." (In other words, "I find you a most undesirable person. I am happier when you're not around me. You're too dumb to learn how to cook anyway.")

This carried over into many of the typically feminine activities in the home. Mom never taught her anything—how to sew, how to line her eyes, how to hem a dress, how to shop, and so on. At the onset of menstruation, Mom tossed a pamphlet through the bathroom door to her. Who was this girl learning about all these years, Mom or herself? Herself! She learned, *I'm not feminine. I can't do anything right with regard to being feminine. I'm worthless!* Then her feeler got stuck. She feels unfeminine at level eight and has for years. She's playing the game with only the top two points on her feeler scale.

Along about age nine or ten, this little girl began to fight back at all this rejection. Now that she had learned to reject herself as a female, she was getting more and more frustrated at her inability to satisfy her need for love. This generated hostility that she directs mainly at herself for being such a loser as a female. But she scatterguns her hostility toward females in general because *they all represent rejection to her*. She has been trained to relate to women by rejecting them first. She anticipates their rejection of her. It seems *normal* to her! If they won't reject her, she will try to *make* them do so. This is the turf on which she is most comfortable (a very miserable comfortable).

Then she got saved. Her old identity died in Christ, and she was born a new woman in Him. But her brain still has all that software in it for feeling hostile toward females. The curvy lady represents the epitome of femininity to her—everything she feels she is not. Curvy ladies are a painful reminder of her own failure. She is tempted to react to this stimulus with rejection and hostility.

When the curvy lady passes into her view, the brain yields a printout. Sin says, "Look at that! *I'll* bet she's wearing more pads than the Chicago Bears!" This is not *her* thought. As the new woman she *now is*, she loves women. God did not spawn a new woman who hates other women. He has written His laws of love "on her heart" (see Heb. 10:16). He has given her a new heart (see Ezek. 36:26). These prophecies have already been fulfilled in born-again people. If she doesn't know this, however, if she believes that God left her a hopeless house divided against herself, spiritual Siamese twins who battle each other constantly, she will likely accept this thought from sin. And once she does that, its thought becomes her's. She is deceived, and she's now sinning in her thought life.

The next step is the rattlesnake routine. Feeler begins to climb. But wait! Remember that her elevator never starts from the lobby. She feels hostile toward women at level eight on her *best* days. With this advantage, sin instantly socks it to her mind again. "Look at that bleached hair! I'd like to jerk it out by its black roots! Women like that make me sick! Worthless little pet housedog!" The power of sin will keep pouring it on her mind as long as she will be sucker enough to sit there and drink it in.

Passing It On

Now, this woman is not being driven by a biological need the way the macho flesh man was. Whereas he may well leave his car at the Evil One's insistence to try to make friends with the curvy lady, our lady is not apt to chase her down and start a street fight. No, she will just sit in her car and fume until her feeler gets to ten.

About this time, the woman's seven-year-old daughter returns to the car from the errand she had run. She has great difficulty closing her car door. Slam, rattle, rattle, rattle. Open up again . . . slam, rattle, rattle. Open up again. Now we have a new printout in Mama's brain. Young female (*an extension of Mama's own self-image*, and she hates herself) can't even close a door right. If you were sin, what would you say to mama now? It will travel up yet another green highway and trigger the thought, *You idiot! Can't you do anything right? Do I have to do everything?* This anger is not directed against the curvy lady, though. There is no danger of damaging Mom's Christian witness with "real" people here. This is only a kid! Much of the restraint is gone. She bellows it out, reaches roughly across her daughter's lap, and slams the door with all the hostility she can release. Wham! Then she starts the car and aims it toward the house. Her jaw is set. Her knuckles are white as she grips the wheel. She tells her daughter to shut up when she meekly tries to apologize. She snaps off the radio that had been playing. They speed toward the house in deathly silence.

Who is this little girl learning about? Is she learning, *Boy, Mom, you are really a hard case!* No, you realize by now that she's learning, *Ugh. I just can't do anything right. I* always *mess up. I* always *cause mom to be upset. And I don't blame her. She has every right to be upset. I'm such a klutz! I hate myself! I wish I were gone! She'd be so much happier if I were just gone. I wish I were dead.* And the sins of the parents are visited "on the children to the third and fourth generations" (Exod. 34:7).

Mom got rejected by her mom. Now she is rejecting her own daughter. The daughter will grow up and reject her own. And where will it stop? I'll tell you where it can stop. At the Cross! This precious sister in Christ can hold a good funeral to all that she used to be and then celebrate the *fact*, not the feeling, of who she *now is*.

She *is* a new creation whom she can love and accept. She has always longed to be a new and different person. Well, congratulations are in order. She *is* a new person. She has simply never been taught who she *now* is as the new woman. When she claims these things as her own, agreeing with God's Word that it is true, and begins to act like it's all true in her, His beautiful healing process will begin. She will be "transformed by the renewing of [her] mind" (Rom. 12:2).

Inferiority Flesh

Next to this lady's car, yet another Christian woman sits waiting in front of the post office. Her child has gone in after the mail from their box. This dear lady was rejected by her dad during childhood. In her case, it resulted from his being a workaholic. He simply never took time to be with her. There was the day she marched in her first parade with the band. She was the fourth one from the right in the clarinet section. She had told him right where to look for her when they came past his store. He missed it. It seems a man had asked him if he could come out to do an estimate, and, of course, he had to go.

There was the time he was going to go out to see some land he was thinking about buying. He promised her she could go along. She had braided her hair all by herself for the big event. She still remembers it. She was seven years old at the time. She sat out on the porch in the swing. She got there ten minutes early because Daddy didn't like her to be late. But he never came. He completely forgot, he said. And he had such a phenomenal memory. Everyone always said so. She never did make much of an impression on him, though. Need I continue?

Out of this relationship with her dad, the little girl learned that she was worthless, unlovely, unattractive to males, unimportant, and nonstimulating, among other yukky things. She felt this way for so long a time that her feeler got choreographed. She had a very low self-esteem. Then she got saved. It was a wonderful experience for her. She *felt* loved for the first time in her life. But alas, the feelings came with a one-year warranty. She slowly but surely gravitated back to her old feelings rut.

Our sister in Christ is now twenty-nine, married, has two kids, is overweight, and is very unhappy with life. When the curvy lady appears on her visual screen, sin says to her, "If only I had been born to look like that. Sigh. Then maybe I'd be more attractive to my husband. Sigh. I don't see why he puts up with me. I'm such a clod!" And *she swallows it hook, line, and sinker.* She is now sinning in her thought life. The more she sits and listens to sin's thoughts, the more depressed she becomes. Then sin says to her, "*I'd* like a doughnut. *I* think I'll just stop in and have one on the way home." And she does! In fact, while she was in there, she *received* the idea to have three. Guess where that idea came from? Are you beginning to see how Satan's agent, sin, works?

If she is to attain victory over her unique version of the flesh, she must recognize that, based on the reality of God's Word, those are not *her* thoughts. They are coming from her enemy, sin, waging war against her mind. She must claim experientially her true identity. She is a godly woman who has God's love written on her heart. She is a lovely creature, a princess, the younger sister of the King of the universe, Jesus. This woman is not the same person who generated those old ways through which sin is now attempting to control her. She is to respond to this depreciation attack against her by thinking, *No! Those are not my thoughts. I am dead to them. They're being fed to me. I choose to act dead to them because God's Word tells me that I am dead to sin. I choose instead to "set my mind on [the reality of] things above," the way things* really *are* (see Figure 6.3 again).

The Fleshly Self-Image

You can see from the development of this Biblical perspective
that each Christian's flesh is essentially his self-image that he has
generated while walking as a rebellious, lost person and then
later as a deceived and controlled saved person. If he has been
successful at getting his need for self-esteem satisfied, he has generated USDA Choice Flesh; if moderately successful, he has an
average self-image — Plain Vanilla Flesh. If he's been unsuccess-
ful, he has Yukky Flesh with its low self-esteem.

USDA Choice Flesh

What is the successful person's self-image? Great! In his life,
he has completely accepted certain "givens" about himself: "I am
as good as anyone else, indeed better than average. I am successful. I am lovable and worthy of respect. I respect myself. I
am secure. I have my life together. I accept myself." I do not intend to imply conceit. He's just secure.

Well, isn't that what we're all looking for? Isn't this what our
culture says is the ultimate goal? Moms and dads pray their
daughters will marry such a man. I want him for a next-door
neighbor. He would probably mow my lawn if I got sick. So why
knock him? I do not knock *him*. I disapprove of his *method* for at-
taining the above. It was all a product of his effort to gain self-
esteem as he *used* the resources over which he was made steward,
the ones God entrusted to him to bring glory to Jesus. He ex-
pended his life to get his need for love and self-esteem satisfied,
perhaps even by living for others, but his covert goal was to feel
good about *himself*. He has successfully played Lord of the Ring.

Just like Saul of Tarsus, this dear "successful" person's self-
esteem is of his *own* doing. It is a righteousness of his own, a
house of cards built on the sandy foundation of his own misuse
of the resources that were entrusted to him by the one who owns
all things, including him. He is to count all his fleshly building
as loss, not having any righteousness that can be called his own
based on his performance (see Phil. 3:7-9). His self-esteem must
now be based on entirely different criteria: (1) who he is as the
new man in Christ, and (2) letting Christ express His life
through him as a "living sacrifice" to do *His* will (see Rom. 12:1).
Only this will bring solid satisfaction. Only this will enable a

person to build a self-image that will be totally impregnable to anything this world can throw at it. This is a self-acceptance built of spiritual materials, not fleshly ones. It is an esteem based on our "righteousness which comes from God on the basis of faith" (Phil. 3:9).

"Homemade" Vanilla Flesh

The "Ordinary Christian" type of flesh is the result of winsome, lose-some experiences with which most of us can identify. An example of this could be the possessing of talent in a specific area such as athletics, music, or mechanical repair. We also have some Yukky Flesh patterns that produce a low yield or even a negative yield, such as being too quick to speak and thus alienating people with whom we would like to establish friendships. This results in loss of love from others, and also loss of self-love.

Whereas Captain Christian up there in the previous example would be scoring himself eight to ten on all the positive characteristics, Ordinary Christian is going to give himself fives and sixes.

Yukky Flesh

The difference between low self-esteem and humility is that low self-esteem concentrates totally on *self*: "What are people thinking about me? How do they think I look? Why am I so dumb!" Humility, on the other hand, concentrates on the welfare of others: "I'll take this back seat so others can sit up there. I hope she's chosen instead of me because I feel she needs that." Low self-esteem and humility often look the same on the outside, but they are poles apart.

Jesus had a healthy self-esteem, but He was humble. Embracing a low self-image is one big fleshwalk. It's concentrating on self constantly. Though it may pass for humility in the Church, it's seen for exactly what it is by God. If the shoe fits, you must hold a good funeral to that, dear one.

Channel #1

No matter which general category of flesh you may fall into, it is all of this world system, not of God. If you keep on listening to those familiar thoughts that seem to be your old sin nature, you will be a pawn in the Evil One's hand. You will be neutral-ized in the spiritual warfare.

Figure 6.4 depicts the believer's being controlled by indwell-ing sin. I have drawn a full circle from the devil, who is in au-thority over the power of sin in the believer's body, through the flesh in the brain, into the mind to: (1) deceive the believer, who then (2) chooses with his will to (3) set his mind on the decep-tion, which (4) results in heightening the emotions, which (5) in-creases the pressure on the will, which (6) chooses to "do the very thing I hate." This behavior then cycles back through Satan, and he thus keeps the believer under his dominance. But remember: we do not have to act on these thoughts that are now foreign to us. We are no longer under sin's control.

I am going to call this "Channel #1." Stay tuned to Channel #1 and be deceived. That's the way the Evil One works, espe-cially on a Christian who believes he has two natures. Satan is capable of talking that Christian into some pretty raunchy be-havior and then justifying his failure by giving him thoughts like, *Well, my old sin nature took over, and I did it again. But that's nor-mal for us Christians*. Deceived!

"The Fleshly Self-Image, Channel #1"

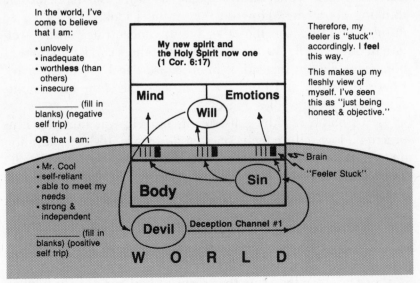

Figure 6.4

Tragically, many high-profile Christians are falling and bringing great harm to the name of Christ. They seem power-less to "life out" the victory they teach. Somehow their Christianity is not working. The reason it's not working is they do not understand their *true identity* and how to offer themselves as a living sacrifice to Christ to live the victorious Christian life *through* them.

Questions for Further Study

1. How does Satan offer up temptation to you that is truly tempting when you really don't want to sin in the first place?

2. Do the sinful thoughts that new creatures in Christ experience *originate* in their minds? Try to explain your answer by using Figure 6.4. After having done so, refer to the two paragraphs above the diagram to check your answer.

3. Try to verbalize what your personal temptations sound like as Satan offers them up in accordance with your flesh.

4. "You will 'life out' whatever you believe to be your true self, your true identity." What does this statement mean to you?

5. Where does your victory lie as a person in Christ, a child of God?

LIVING LIKE A
NEW CREATION

The changes in my marriage since Anabel and I began to let Jesus live through us are astounding. Listen again to Anabel:

> If only I could express to you how different my life is from what it was seventeen years ago as I seriously considered ending it all after twenty years of living in a hell on earth. Bill tries so hard to make up for all the years of lashing out at me from his frustration with himself. I could wish for any woman the marriage I have today.
>
> I could mention many things, but I'll just share one way in which things have changed. He brings me things, little things. Like when he's out running in the mornings, he might bring me a little wild flower he picked. I'll find it floating face up in a juice glass on the window sill over my sink as I turn on the light to fix breakfast. I love it!
>
> Do you know what it says to me? "I was thinking about you. I *know* you. I know what you like. I've *listened* to you to discover what you like. I'm *interested* in you. *Your* needs are important to me. You're not just someone who can meet *my* needs."
>
> But, oh, there is so much more than just the change in Bill's behavior toward me. Even though that has been wonderful, I would have still been a prisoner to my own unique version of the flesh. But I'm free! Free from losing the inner wrestling match. And free from *listening* to and *receiving* the inner condemnation I lived with for forty years! It's still there; Satan hasn't given up. But I'm much better at recognizing his tactics now, and I set my mind on the truth about myself from God's Word.

How in the world can Anabel say those kind things about me after the way I've treated her? It's a result of God's giving her the grace to forgive me; the result of her being able to "set her mind" on how secure and accepted she is in Him, which means she can consistently rest in Him; the result of Christ's living through me to radically change my behavior; and the result of my resting in my total acceptance in Him, being freed from fighting for survival in my role as a male. Oh, yes, we still struggle at times, but we have entered into God's rest (see Matt. 11:28, 29).

You Can Keep a Good Man Down

We have already seen in Romans 7:15-25 how the law of sin will control the believer to keep him captive. Sin continually condemns many Christians in their thought life. This is especially true for those with perfectionistic flesh. Sin hammers these dear people constantly, "telling" them that they are failing because they cannot achieve perfect results. I'll now use the same passage to accomplish a second goal, documenting the believer's true identity in Christ.

Let's take this passage verse by verse and apply our hypothesis that the Christian person is *actually, literally* holy in his heart and see if it will fly. Romans 7 is usually thought of as the most depressing, defeating chapter in the New Testament. I propose to take this passage and prove to your discerning mind that the person in Christ is literally godly. Then we'll see how to make our behavior consistent with that reality.

Romans 7:15 says this,

> For that which I am doing, I do not understand; for I am not practicing what I would like to do, but I am doing the very thing I hate.

We have here a person whose *desire* is to obey God, but who lacks the power to live it out somehow. He sins, but he hates it. The first point I wish to make, then is this: what kind of "heart" does this person have? What do I mean by heart? I mean the deepest, innermost dynamic of what drives this man; his deep desire. Does this man rejoice over his sinning, or is he miserable because of it? He is miserable, and the reason is that he's powerless to make his performance line up with his heart. His heart is *good*. If his heart were only semi-good, he would have a tolerance for sinful performance. If he had two "natures" as we have been taught, one good and one evil, this verse would read entirely differently. It would read to accommodate the two desires like so:

> I understand very well what I am doing; for I am practicing what I *like* to do. Half the time I do evil things, and the other half I practice good. I delight to do both and find no conflict in this, as it is perfectly normal for me to satisfy both my "natures."

Such is not the case with Paul, however. He is miserable because he cannot bring his performance into line with his holy nature.

Let's go on to verse 18: "For I know that nothing good dwells in me, that is, in my flesh." Note, he doesn't say that *he* is no good, but that nothing good *dwells* in his *flesh*. Now, the Holy Spirit dwells in his earthsuit, and He is certainly something good. So Paul must be speaking of the old, green highways definition of the term *flesh*, and truly, "nothing good" *dwells* there.

Please note though, that he does not say *he* is not good. The remainder of the verse states "for the wishing is present in me, but the doing of the good is not." He is a *good man* who cannot find the power to "life out" his goodness.

I believe I would be too charitable to say that most Bible teachers take the position that Christians are "half good and half evil" as new creatures in Christ. What most imply is that we are 90 percent evil and 10 percent good. Many are even harder on us than that. Their messages to Christians imply that we are 100 percent evil and 0 percent good, citing "in me dwells no good thing" as "proof," failing to complete the verse, which states, "in me dwells no good thing, that is, *in my flesh*." Of course there is "no good thing" in my flesh (old ways), but the person in Christ is now "the one who *wishes* to do *good*." We're the good guys! Or they cite "The heart of man is desperately wicked" from Jeremiah 17:9. Of course that man's heart is desperately wicked; the prophet was speaking of the "old man" in this Old Testament passage. That is not the new person. The new creature in Christ has had a heart transplant! We deeply desire to do good.

A Fly in the "Anointment"

Paul continues,

> But if I am doing the very thing I do not wish, I am no longer the one doing it, but sin which dwells in me (v. 20).

As we have already seen, Paul identifies the culprit, the source of his poor performance. This thing is somehow controlling this good man and deceiving him into "acting sinfully." And you will recall that the power of indwelling sin will deceive the believer in his mind by sending him thoughts with first-person singular pronouns through the flesh, attempting to control him against his true nature.

Paul says,

> I find then the principle that evil is present in me, the one who wishes to do good (v. 21).

Evil is *present* in this man. This doesn't say that *he* is evil, but that he (the one who desires to do good) has evil present in him. That's a very real and crucial distinction. He is a good man.

If you have a gold crown on your tooth, does that make you a gold mine? No, you have gold *present* in you. If you get a splinter in your foot, does that make you a totem pole? No, you have wood *present* in you. Neither is this good man anything other than good because he has evil *present* in him, according to this passage. But many Christians have misinterpreted it.

Your Body Is Not Saved

Paul continues further, saying,

> For I joyfully concur with the law of God in the inner man (v. 22).

This man totally agrees with, loves, and desires the law of God in his true identity.

> But I see a different law in the members of my body (v. 23).

Aha! Now we identify the *location* of the problem. Sin still resides in the *body*. It is not in the soul or the spirit. Those two parts are the righteous new man (see 2 Cor. 5:14-21). But technically, the body has not been saved yet: later in the epistle, Paul says that we are "waiting eagerly for . . . the redemption of our body" (Rom. 8:23). It is still earthbound and destined to return to the dust. It will *be* saved one day at the resurrection. It will *be* transformed into a new, glorified body (see 1 Cor. 15:42-44). Our bodies aren't evil, but they are earthy. I call the body the "vehicle of vulnerability." It is vulnerable to being used by the evil one if we submit to him.

Continuing on with verse 23,

> . . . but I see a different law in the members of my body waging war against the law of my mind.

What sort of law is the "law of my mind," godly or evil? Godly! Your mind *has* to be pure and good for there to be a battle. If there is a war going on, can the opponents be on the same side? No. They must be in total opposition to each other. A "new person in Christ" is a "partaker of the divine nature" (2 Pet. 1:3, 4). He "has the laws of God written on his mind." This man's mind is *good*. He has a "sound mind," "the mind of Christ," or there would be no war.

> Wretched man that I am! Who will set me free from the body of this death? (v. 24).

The word *wretched* does not mean evil; it means unhappy. This man is stating that he is terribly unhappy living like this, as will be any person who has only one nature, a godly one, and who has not claimed his true identity in Christ. But — praise God! — look at his answer to his own question in verse 25: "Thanks be to God through Jesus Christ our Lord!" He's free! But he will never experience it if he walks according to the flesh, only if he walks in the Spirit. His identification in the death, burial, and resurrection with Christ has set him free.

> So then, on the one hand I myself with my [sound] mind am serving the law of God [the law of love], but on the other, with my flesh [the "old ways"] the law of sin.

When he chooses to walk in the Spirit (in his true identity), he serves the law of love, but when he is deceived into walking after the flesh, he is serving the law of sin. He doesn't *have* to sin. He is free to obey God through Christ's indwelling life.

Paul then goes on in the next chapter to explain how we, as new people in Christ, are a battleground in which God fights His archenemy, the devil. Note how many verses in chapter 8 pit sin against God, the Spirit versus the flesh, and so on. But make no mistake about it, Christian, we are free to obey God. "For the law of the Spirit of life in Christ Jesus *has set you free* from the law of sin and of death" (Rom. 8:2, emphasis added). And "there is therefore now no condemnation for those who are in Christ Jesus" (Rom. 8:1).

You are literally a brand-new person in Him, a good person who loves Jesus and deeply desires to submit to His Kingship. The Kingdom of heaven has arrived. It's in us! Let's turn Him loose to reign in us by acting dead to sin and alive to God!

Concentrate on Starting, Not Stopping

Now that the deception, the "walking according to the flesh" pattern, has been identified, let's trust the Holy Spirit together to put some practical handles on *how* to implement God's provision for victory. As with every spiritual principle, this victory will not be so much a matter of fighting *against* the power of the Evil One, but rather a matter of *starting up* a new method of walking, moment by moment, experiencing Christ as your very life while simultaneously you "act dead" to those thoughts that will be served up to your mind through the flesh in the brain. The Word says you are "dead to [the power of] sin" (Rom. 6:11). To make this an experiential reality, you must *act* dead to it regardless of feelings.

Let's look at just a few of the many astounding and glorious things God has to say about our true identity, the new people we are in Christ.

I Am Holy

Many can identify with having learned in this world that they are unlovely, worthless, inadequate, or insecure. But if God says that "old you" died and the new resurrected you is holy, even though the world won't agree, what are you? Whom will you believe? You say, "But I don't *act* holy." Well, I hope this will change radically as you read this book, but the Word doesn't state that you always act holy anyway. We're not discussing performance; we're discussing identity.

Some may ask, "But isn't it just that God *sees* us as holy?" No, that would be saying that God somehow deceived Himself by pretending we are holy when the fact is that we're grubby. That can't be the case, dear Christian! God told Peter in the vision on the rooftop, "Don't you call unholy what God has called holy" (Acts 10:15, author's paraphrase). God has called *you* holy: ". . . who have been sanctified in Christ Jesus, saints [holy ones] by calling, with all who in every place call upon the name of our Lord Jesus Christ, their Lord and ours" (1 Cor. 1:2).

I Am Accepted

Are you accepted or rejected? You say, "Well, I *feel* like the other women in the women's group at church sometimes reject me." Okay, so perhaps they reject you. Did God promise you they wouldn't? No, He just said they shouldn't. But He did promise you that *He* wouldn't. Has He? No. Will He? No! He can't. How do we know? Because He *said* so. "I will never desert you, nor will I ever forsake you" (Heb. 13:5). Believe Him. You *are* accepted. "Wherefore, accept one another, just as Christ also accepted us to the glory of God" (Rom. 15:7).

I Am Blameless

Is God holding grudges against you for the times you've failed Him in the past? No! "You were dead in sins, and your sinful desires were not yet cut away. Then he gave you a share in the very life of Christ, for he forgave all your sins" (Col. 2:13, TLB). He has declared you blameless before Him. "That He might present to Himself the Church in all her glory, having no spot or wrinkle or any such thing; but that she should be holy and blameless" (Eph. 5:27). "Just as He chose us in Him before the foundation of the world, that we should be holy and blameless before Him" (Eph. 1:4).

I Am Already in Heaven

You are actually seated in heaven, according to God's Word, experiencing God's rest (above your circumstances). You are secure, loved, and treasured. "And God rais*ed* us up with Him, and seat*ed* us with Him in the heavenly places, in Christ Jesus" (Eph. 2:6, emphasis added). It's to be *believed* continually, Christian, not *felt* continually.

I Am Complete

You've already "made it" with God. You are complete in Christ. How are you going to improve on perfect? I didn't say it; He did: "*In* Him, you have been made complete" (Col. 2:10).

I Am Totally Forgiven

Are you guilty or forgiven there in heaven? Can anything guilty be in heaven? "And when you *were* dead in your transgressions and the uncircumcision of your flesh [lost], He *made* you alive together with Him, *having forgiven* us *all* our transgressions" (Col. 2:13, emphasis added). You *are* forgiven—totally!

I Am a Conqueror Over Evil

You are no longer inadequate but more than a conqueror. You *are* victorious through Him (see Rom. 8:37). The circumstances may not always support this view, but the Word does. Whose scorecard are you reading, anyway? We are resting in *His* victory. It's a mind rest, not an emotion. Meditate on it! Appropriate it!

I Am Not Condemned

"There is therefore *now* no condemnation for those who are in Christ Jesus" (Rom. 8:1, emphasis added). You're not condemned! Yes, the Lord will condemn your sinful performance, and you will experience the accompanying conviction. This must be dealt with in a Biblical manner, but the verse clearly states that God will never condemn your person, your identity; only your sins.

Do you see who you are? I understand that you may not *feel* like this. Your feeler won't agree with the message, but your mind can. God's Word says that these beautiful things are now the fabric from which the new you has been cut. You must simply accept God's statements about "any man in Christ" at face value and step forward as if this were all true about *you*.

Don't be intimidated by your emotions and the "logical arguments" that are continually being served up to your mind by indwelling sin. "For though we walk in the flesh, we do not war according to the flesh, for the weapons of our warfare are not of the flesh, but divinely powerful for the destruction of fortresses. We are destroying *speculations* and every lofty thing raised up against the knowledge of God, and we are taking *every thought* captive to the obedience of Christ" (2 Cor. 10:3-5, emphasis added).

The Word says in 2 Corinthians 5:14-21 that all Christians died in Christ and were reborn as different people who are not to live to get their needs met, but for His service. It says that we are no longer known by our old identity, but by who we *now are*. "We are ambassadors for Christ" (v. 20). Ambassadors are citizens of their home country who reside in a foreign land as representatives of their homeland. That's us! We are spiritual citizens of heaven who live on Satan's turf as representatives of our Father God.

Commands Are Not Optional

In essence, God says in Colossians 3:1-4a, "Now, then, Son, I want you to understand what your true identity is and the method I have designed to enable you to live it out. If you *have been* raised up with Christ, keep seeking the things above where Christ is, because you're *in* Him there, too, seated at the right hand of God. Set your mind on the things above, not on the things that are on earth."

What "things above" should you think about? Well, don't dwell on golden streets and mansions. That won't transform you. Rather, see yourself relaxing there in Christ. All your needs are met. Your Father has everything under control. He is totally accepting you and loving you. You are a son or daughter in the Father's forever family. You are holy and blameless before Him. You have become a "partaker of the divine nature." *Think* on these things. Pump this truth through and through your mind. It's reality!

"When Christ, who is our life . . ." (Col. 3:4). Wow! *He is* your life! Right now, *He* is the only life you have. If He were ever to leave you, we'd know it right off, because your earthsuit would fall over dead. Your soul and spirit could not reside in it without His life, because your old life died in Him at Calvary.

Since Christ is your life, wouldn't it be a normal thing for you to let Him express His life through you? Jesus is the only one who ever lived a victorious life, and the indwelling Holy Spirit is the way He can now express that life through you. That wouldn't make you another Jesus, as some teach, any more than you were another Adam when you used to be in Adam. It's just that now, instead of Adam's life of self-service, you have Christ's life of other-service. It's His Life we have, not His personality.

On the other hand, if you don't let Him live through you, you are "presenting the members of your body to [the power of] sin" (Rom. 6:13). Your motivation will be to get your needs met. You will be depending on yourself. That's the same "life" a lost person lives.

Don't assume, either, that Christ's living through you means you're to be passive. You're not to sit there until you *feel* Him take over. He will express the same life through you that He lived through His own earthsuit and personality, a life of obedience to the Father. He lived a life of service, not survival. But we have to *act* it out, believing it's Christ doing it through us, by faith.

First, His life must manifest itself in and be most noticeable in your *own home*, to your family. Next, it must be obvious to the brethren. Jesus said, "Your strong love for each other will prove to the world that you are my disciples" (John 13:35, TLB). Finally, it must be demonstrated to the lost. Unless the lost can see Christ in and through you as you interact with your own physical and spiritual families, your words to them will be a brass gong. As you allow Christ to live through you, you can actually be victorious in this. You can *act* lovingly.

Please listen. Such a life of victory is open for you to appropriate as your own. God is in fact *commanding* all Christians to "set their minds" on the way things really are. That's not optional; it's a direct command from your God to you. *Think*, meditate, attend to, contemplate. You are a new person resting in heaven (side B), while simultaneously here on planet earth,

Christ is expressing His loving life through you (side A; see Figure 7.1). We'll represent this "mind set" with a series of lines and label it Channel #2, the *reality* channel.

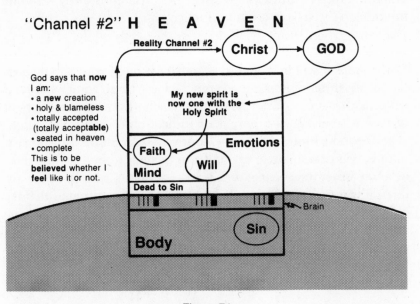

Figure 7.1

How to Set Your Mind

"Setting your mind" *must* be attainable or God wouldn't command you to do it. In fact, you do it every day. Let me illustrate.

Imagine you are walking down a gravel road in Arkansas. Put a cool creek bubbling alongside the road. Hear the water gurgling? Let's make it an early morning in the month of May. Put a red bird in a tree, and have him singing. Imagine a light ground mist on the meadow across the road. Now put a couple of cows in the pasture. See how easily you can choose to let your mind get caught up in this scene?

Now let's change the imagery. I want you to set your mind on eating a hamburger at your favorite burger restaurant. It needs just a tad more seasoning. Put some on it. Now take another bite. Ah, that's better. Take a swig of your favorite beverage. Let's make it a really hot summer day, and you're dying for a drink. Feel it going down? Um, so refreshing.

Change the scene again. Set your mind on driving your car down the freeway. Let's make it night, and you're out in the country. A truck is stalled on the shoulder ahead. See the flares? Smell the diesel fumes as you whiz by? You constantly set your mind, don't you? It's a daily practice.

Bringing Heaven to Earth

Perhaps it will help you to visualize yourself seated in heaven if you can think of it as a place much closer than "somewhere out beyond the stars." The Scriptures teach that the direction of heaven is upward, but there is no indication it is 40 million light years beyond Pluto. Quite the contrary, Abraham and the rich man carried on a conversation from heaven to hell within sight of each other (see Luke 16:19-31). I don't know how far up heaven is, but it's not going to be heresy for us to pretend that it's only one inch above the earth. That's up! Study Figure 7.2 to see yourself at rest in heaven while facing life on earth simultaneously, allowing Christ to express *His* life through you. This is

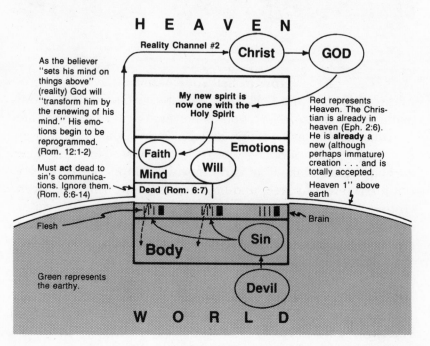

Figure 7.2

"setting your mind on things above" in a practical sense. Set your mind (by faith) that you are holy, blameless, righteous, and accepted, with all your needs (not greeds) supplied. Simultaneously set your mind that Christ is expressing His life through you to meet your daily circumstances. You and I are not to worry about life. "Be anxious for nothing" (Phil. 4:6). That's not something to be *felt*; it's the act of setting your mind. You can't set your feeler, but let your feeler be God's problem.

Now let's build on our new picture of where heaven is. Visualize yourself as being in heaven (one inch off the floor). You are relaxing in Christ near the right elbow of God the Father. How many troubles do you have there? How nervous are you? How badly do you hurt emotionally? How rejected are you? How worried are you about what tomorrow holds? Isn't it peaceful there? While you are resting there, imagine the Father reaching around you with His strong right arm and snuggling you up to His chest. Can you smell how clean His robe is and feel its texture on your cheek? Come on now, you guys with your feeler stuck so much that you're uncomfortable with the picture I'm painting. If your feeler won't cooperate, rain on it! *Set your mind on this scene anyway.* Let God worry about taking care of your stuck feeler in His own good time. Just set your mind on this scene because this *is* reality, Channel #2. Pause now and "set your mind on things above" for *five whole minutes*. Go! (Sin just said to you, "Oh, I won't do that right now. I get his point. I'll just read on.") Come on now. Do what I asked you. Please. You'll love what will happen inside you.

Friend, what if you set your mind on the reality I've described for about three or four hours each day? Not all at once, but fifteen seconds here, a minute there, and so on. What would happen to you? You'd be "transformed by the renewing of your mind." Because, you see, this process would leave you four hours less time to set your mind on Channel #1. And what would happen to those green highways in your brain because of that disuse? The same thing that happened to your high school algebra. They would dissipate. Tell me, by what process did you forget your algebra? Did you try to "overcome" it by attacking it, or did you simply "set your mind" on something else and the forgetting took care of itself?

Do you see it? One of the critical keys to victory over your flesh is consistently "setting your mind" in the reality of Channel #2. Don't concentrate your energies on fighting against setting your mind on Channel #1. That would be concentrating on "death," which would effectively cut you off from your life, Christ. You are dead to Channel #1, so why fight against it? Simply *act* as though you're dead to it.

Being dead to sin, however, is not sufficient by itself. You are simultaneously alive to God. Victory lies in concentrating your energies in generating Channel #2 thoughts with your sound mind. Start 'em up! See yourself seated in Christ, resting while in this circumstance. See yourself loved, totally accepted, godly and holy. This is *your* life, "for . . . your life is hidden with Christ in God" (Col. 3:3). Your obedience to truth will result in light conquering darkness. *This isn't a world-system, counterfeit power of positive thinking or Eastern religious meditation. It's the Bible. God didn't give you an option of setting your mind or not as you choose. He has commanded you to do it.* And when you do it, you're walking in *reality*. When you choose not to do it, you are walking in *deception*, controlled through the thoughts by the Evil One in Channel #1.

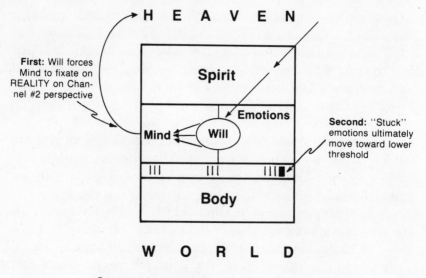

Demonstrating how the threshold of the emotions gets "unstuck" through "setting the mind on things above."

Figure 7.3

Your Emotions Will Begin to be Reprogrammed

Set your mind on reality and the Holy Spirit will gradually begin to supernaturally lower the stuck threshold of your feeler down toward a more normal position. This will give you more points to play the ballgame with on your emotional Richter Scale (see Figure 7.3). You'll be much more able to tolerate situations that formerly would have led to certain spiritual defeat.

Will the Real Hypocrite Please Stand Up

Since God says the Channel #2 perspective is truth, what does that make the Channel #1 perspective? Deception. It's based on the false premise that the old man had resurrection power, that he somehow arose from the dead and continues to wage war against the new man.

If you are embracing and living out Channel #1, you are living a lie. You are acting as if Channel #1 were reality and Channel #2 an idealistic pipe dream that you can't seem to make "come true." Therefore, you are "pretending" Channel #1 is your identity, when in fact Channel #2 is your identity! *You are pretending to be what you are not.* And you know what God has to say about folks who pretend to be what they aren't? He calls them *hypocrites.* (Jesus called the Pharisees hypocrites because they claimed they were holy, when in fact they were not.)

The devil's definition of a hypocrite is "anyone who acts contrary to how he *feels.*" It's all based on emotion. Try to act in a manner contrary to how you feel and he will accuse you in your mind of being a phony. He is "the accuser of the brethren" (see Rev. 12:10).

It will seem like self-accusation, however, because again, the thoughts will be presented to your mind by the power of sin with first person singular pronouns: "Why, I can't tell my wife that I love her and that I'm thankful for what she does for me when I don't *feel* like it. That would make me a hypocrite!" Christians swallow that line because they don't know it is originating with the accuser. Most of them never break through the deception to victory. They sit there and wait, hoping the Lord will somehow change their *feelings* so they can act accordingly without "being a hypocrite." Channel #1!

Now, what if you would simply *act* as if Christ were expressing *His* life through your personality and earthsuit to bypass the flesh and speak loving, encouraging, tender words to your wife and children. What if you let Him use your arms to reach out in love by giving them a hug or a pat on the back? You would be acting as if Christ actually were your life. You would be acting like something is true that *is* true, wouldn't you? Would you be a hypocrite, or would you be acting like *what you are*? You would be living obediently to the Word of God by faith. Do you see it? Ignore how you *feel* and the accusations served up to your mind that are contrary to your true identity. You'll be experiencing Christ as life, letting Him filter His life through your personality.

Practical Applications

Let's put the rubber on the road and apply these truths to some everyday situations. Consider a man [me] who has a wide, green highway in his brain for selfishness and self-indulgence. He often finds it difficult to give of his time to his wife and kids. He experiences persistent thoughts (served up to his mind by the power of sin) and feelings of resistance when any of them make demands on "his" time. Although the illustration I'm about to use may sound a little silly to you, it illustrates an intense problem for him.

His wife requests that when he mows the yard, would he please use the catcher on the lawnmower and bag the cuttings. You see, she's really saying, "Husband, please love me by bagging the grass." This is the way she's spelling love today. But sin says to him, "It's such a hassle to bag the grass! It takes twice as long! I wish she'd get off my case!" It's always worse if his feeler is acting up on that particular day. Hey, this is Anabel and Bill! This describes one of my flesh patterns.

How am I going to experience victory in this situation? It won't do me much good to practice seeing myself seated in heaven. That won't get much grass cut and bagged. I need some performance! Thus, I will employ the side A truth of Christ's being my life. I will let Him filter His life through me by cutting and bagging the grass. I *know* He wants to do it, because it really does need to be done. It would be ugly to "windrow" it, because it is pretty high. Anabel's request was quite reasonable. Besides, He has told me to love her as He loves *His* bride.

I start the mower and begin to push it across the lawn, but *I simultaneously choose with my will to set my mind that He is mowing the lawn through me.* It's just a matter of believing that He is and acting as if He is. *It's all done by faith and obedience.* You keep concentrating on your method of operation, faith and obedience.

As I walk along, I generate in my mind, "Well, Lord, it's really neat to not have to mow and bag today. I'm sure glad you let me off the hook by doing it all for me. What a neat thing it is to rest while I work. You are something else! Oh, oh, Lord, the bag's full. We'd better stop and empty it. That baby sure fills up in a hurry, doesn't it? Man, I'm sure glad I don't have to empty the grass into those bags. That's the part I hate the most! Boy, You sure do make short work of it. Yessir, it's a real pleasure to watch You do the work through me." That's the "fellowship of His sufferings" (Phil. 3:10). Notice that it's *His* sufferings, not mine.

You say, "Come on, Gillham, what a dumb story! Let's move on to some illustrations of claiming the abundant life. Get on to the story of when you went to the big meeting at the convention center and saw a guy's leg grow a quarter of an inch and then everybody swung on the chandeliers." Well, I enjoy a little chandelier swinging, but the abundant life is not always doing one-and-a-halfs off the ceiling fixtures. *The abundant life is being able to spend Saturday morning mowing and bagging grass for your wife without getting resentful over it. That* is the abundant life for me. That's victory over my flesh.

Someone says, "That's what you call sufferings? Bagging grass? How hokey can you get!" I guess suffering is a relative thing. But yes, I confess that initially, bagging grass was suffering to me. It's no longer such, as I have been "transformed [in this area] by the renewing of my mind." I even bag the grass when Anabel is gone out of town. I enjoy it. My feeler's unstuck on this one.

Now that we've seen an illustration in which the believer employs side A of our identity in Christ (Christ's life through me), let's develop an example in which the believer will appropriate the truth that he is in Christ (side B).

Suppose you are a woman with six-lane, green highways for feeling inferior and rejected. Your feeler is stuck at about a seven on each of these. You are a teacher in a large elementary school. The state teacher's meeting is this weekend, and you had so hoped to travel to it with three ladies who teach in your building. You get the word, however, that they have arranged to invite another woman because one of them thought it would be fun to have her along, which means that she's more fun to be with than you are. Do you feel rejected? Yes! Have you been rejected? Yes, by them you sure have. Would this be apt to make anyone's feeler go up a few points on feeling rejected? Yes. The trouble is, though, that you've got only three points of tolerance on your Richter Scale. This is going to be a tough one to "turn over to the Lord." Do you also feel inferior to the other woman? Yes. Are you? According to the world's view, yes. According to *reality*, no.

Now, this calls for appropriating side B, setting your mind on resting in heaven in Christ, totally accepted and secure in His love for you. You must *instantly* fight to set your mind. Sin will flood your mind with thoughts such as, *I'm such a yukky person. I'm such a Delberta Dumb. It's no wonder they didn't invite me, I'm such a klutz! I hardly blame them. I seem to have such a talent for casting a wet blanket over any party. Oh, if I were only different!* These "beat on myself" thoughts would be served up only to certain women with this unique sort of flesh.

The woman having self-pity green highways would experience thoughts from sin such as, "Well, after all I've done for them! It'll be a cold day when I ever volunteer to take *their* playground duty when they have a sore throat. Imagine inviting Elsie! That clod always manages to worm her way in. God, You sure have a funny way of treating Your friends. You always seem to make it difficult for me to keep up my faith. Others always get the breaks, and they don't try half as hard as I do. Sometimes I wonder if it's worth all the effort to serve You!" This woman has fleshly patterns to blame others when her needs are not met, while the first woman accepts self-blaming thoughts for the deficiency. It's also very common for a person to experience a combination of these thoughts.

In either case, you must *instantly* begin to generate counterproductive thoughts to these based on truth in Channel #2, while simultaneously claiming what the Scripture states. You are dead to the power of sin that's feeding you those negative thoughts. If you don't, your feeler is going to break the sound barrier. Instantly think, *I am relaxing in Christ at the right hand of the Father. I'm so glad it's not a zillion light years away, Lord, but right here in this room! Oh, I'm loved and accepted!* Imagine yourself snuggled up against His chest. Feel His strong, reassuring arms about you. Are you insecure there? Ha! Are you inferior? Never. No one in Christ is either superior or inferior. First Corinthians 12 makes it clear that eyeballs are equal to elbows in the body of Christ, and you're not inferior to anyone. Confess the truth—aloud if opportunity permits.

Life or Death Matter

Set your mind on these truths. Choose with your will to force your mind to generate appropriate, Biblical, productive, true thoughts while refusing to accept sin's thoughts fed through the brain to your mind. Force yourself to keep at this five minutes, ten minutes, whatever time is necessary until the "attack" of sin's thoughts begins to ease off. If he tries to crank it up again, you crank up again with thoughts counterproductive to his. You see, *it's the setting of your mind in Channel #2 that will enable you to experience being dead to Channel #1.* As I said earlier, it would be a fatal mistake to try to concentrate on being alert to recognize sin's thoughts to you so you could become more skilled at rejecting them. That would be concentrating on *death*, which would effectively cut you off from *life*. Generating therapeutic, Biblical thoughts and setting your mind on these is what will make you more and more victorious over the world, the flesh, and the devil.

You're going to be "transformed by the renewing of your mind" (Rom. 12:2). You'll begin to mature *experientially* into more of what you *already are* in Christ. Your emotions will begin to settle down into the normal Christian ballpark, and the ultimate outcome will be the emergence of godly character that will evolve out of your godly nature and godly behavior.

Watchman Nee, our beautiful Christian brother who used to wear a Chinese earthsuit, made a powerful statement years ago. He said that all knowledge is the outgrowth of obedience; everything else is just information. In other words, you can *believe* the truths taught in this book. Yet, they can still remain just *informa-*

tion to you. If you would convert this information into *knowledge*, you must *obey* it. You must grit your teeth and hold a good funeral, celebrating the after-the-fact death of the old man.

So, start setting your mind. Your character will take on the properties of Christ. The fruits of the Spirit will begin to emerge from you as a *natural product* of your obedience. You don't see the branches on a grape vine straining and groaning to produce grapes. They simply abide, and the life of the vine produces the fruit. That is what you will see happening to you when you begin to appropriate your true identity in Christ. Praise His name!

Questions for Further Study

1. What does it mean to say that the old man died in Christ? Of what significance is this to you?

2. What are some of the attributes that God has given to those who are in Christ that are especially meaningful to you?

3. Once you begin to understand these Biblical truths, of what importance is it that you set your mind on these truths as they apply to you?

4. Look again at the section titled "Practical Applications," and then determine an area of your life that is a particular struggle. Make practical application for it using what you've learned thus far. Write this out. It will help you grasp the principles more firmly.

EIGHT

HANDLING YOUR EMOTIONS

In the last chapter, we saw how it's possible to live like a new creation. But maybe you're wondering how to deal with your emotions. Perhaps you can relate to the following:

> I have given until I don't *feel* like I can give anymore. There are babies and bottles and diapers and beds to make, and dinners and dishes and baths, and then when I fall into bed I'm supposed to be the great lover girl. I *feel* like I've gone under for the third time! How do I deal with these feelings?
>
> Something comes over me and I just let it all go at once! I have this hot temper, and I can't control it. I've always been this way. No matter how hard I try, I can't overcome it! I go totally out of control. I *feel* like it's hopeless.
>
> I don't know what's wrong with me. I tell myself that I'll never let it happen again, but then when we're alone and I *feel* his nearness, I just feel like putty in his hands. I wind up doing it all over again. Help me! Please help me!

What's the role of my emotions? God gave them to me, so they must be good to have. I'd hate to go through life without them or go through eternity unable to feel the euphoria of being in the Savior's presence. But here on earth, my emotions have such a powerful influence on me to violate the will of God at times. The problem is that they respond readily to circumstances, but sometimes painfully slowly to spiritual truth.

How do I deal with my emotions? That's the question I'll address in this chapter. Through carefully studying it, you will gain solid answers you may have sought for years. Thousands of Christians have already gained victory over being controlled by their emotions through the simple teaching in this chapter.

To illustrate how to handle emotions, I'm going to tell a story about a man-eating bear. I am indebted to Chuck Solomon for the initial idea of the story. However, I will take the scenario and greatly elaborate on it, establishing a hierarchy of reactions and then applying the illustration to walking in the Spirit.

An Invitation to Dinner

Let's say you are a stranger visiting Alaska. You're out in the wilderness with no one around. A man-eating bear lives in these parts, and he has just spotted your earthsuit on his turf. He's eight feet tall and weighs six hundred pounds. About a month ago, he ate one of your friends and left only his belt buckle and cowboy boots. He's as mean as a junkyard dog. At the moment, he is occupying himself with running at top speed toward your earthsuit! It's going to take him about ten seconds to close the gap between the two of you and invite you to lunch. Depending on the size of your earthsuit, you are about to become either an hors d'oeuvre or a meal.

Let's draw a picture of this scene (see Figure 8.1). We'll put an eye on your earthsuit so you can see the bear. The sunlight bounces off the bear, through the eye, and up the optic nerve to the brain, where you get a printout of him as he runs toward you. The moment the image of that running bear appears on your picture tube, mind and emotions, which have been sort of sitting there lazily watching TV, come to attention. Instantly,

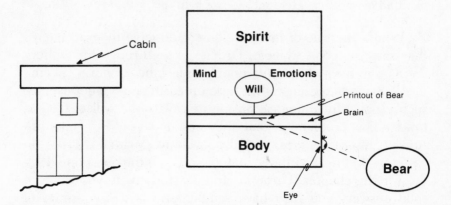

Figure 8.1

mind is going to trigger off a data retrieval system, and up out of the memory banks comes all data relevant to this stimulus.

There are things in your memory banks about bears that you are not going to retrieve at this point, information such as *Bears hibernate in winter.* Instead, you're going to retrieve stuff like *Bears eat meat, and I am meat; running is an option, but bears can run faster than people—however, I could be running while I generate more options; climbing a tree's no good, since he'd just eat me in the treetop.* But then you spot a little cabin through the trees, and mind says, "I can run into that cabin!"

All these options are recommended by your mind to your will at varying levels of intensity according to how strongly mind believes the option will solve the problem. Will is then going to have to choose from among the options presented.

Meanwhile, feeler is getting in on the action. Feeler's going to generate but one emotion appropriate to this situation: fear! On a scale of one to ten, that's a ten! Thus, feeler socks it to will at level ten: "I *feel* like that bear's going to eat me alive, so get moving!" Now, feeler is a tremendous motivator to will. When feeler is talking tens, will is heavily influenced to submit to its demands.

Being thus motivated by both mind and emotions, your will quickly chooses to command the brain to make the muscles propel the earthsuit into the cabin as fast as the legs will move, and they'll be empowered by special rocket fuel injected into the carburetor by adrenal glands at feeler's direction. Feeler has the God-given ability to bypass having to get will's permission to trigger adrenaline flow into the bloodstream. Earthsuit then covers the forty yards to the cabin in 4.6 seconds establishing a new world's record for the forty in cowboy boots.

Now, this cabin is constructed of railroad ties bolted to-gether—even the roof. It's built like a fort. It's also covered with vines, however, so you can't discern its construction. The instant you get inside, you slam the door, which is made of cured-oak bridge timbers three inches thick. You drop a huge wooden bar into a cradle behind the door, and when you do, you instantly become safe in the cabin.

Just as you drop the bar in place, the bear, who was right on your heels and closing fast, slams his nose into the locked door. It stops him cold. He raises up and puts an eye to the lone window (which has no glass, by the way). His head is so big that he can get only one eye to the window at a time. He sees you in there and goes absolutely bananas with rage! He begins to try to rip the cabin apart to get at the nut inside this big husk. (You can relax, now. I'm not going to let him in.) Being a stranger to these parts, you have no knowledge of this cabin's construction and the exterior vines and inner darkness don't help. If I'm a fly on the cabin wall watching you, I'm going to see you plastered against the back wall of the cabin, fearfully awaiting what you fully believe is the inevitable. You are about to get eaten alive by that bear!

But wait a minute. You're safe in the cabin, remember? You could lie down on the floor and catch up on your daily Bible readings, since you're going to be there for a while with nothing to do. Ah, but the problem is that you don't *know* you're safe. Feeler is saying to will, "I feel like that bear is going to burst in here and eat me and that's a fourteen!" Mind, being thus influenced by feeler's intensity, says, "Well, since I *feel* so strongly about this matter, I *believe* that my emotions are telling the truth. I believe I'm going to get eaten by the bear, and that's an eight!" Will, having no input to the contrary, chooses to command brain to make muscles *act* like a man who is about to get eaten by a bear, and there you are doing an imitation of wallpaper.

Do you see that you could actually die of a heart attack in the cabin and never benefit from your safety? You are safe and you don't even know it.

Let's examine this situation and what needs to happen in four steps, beginning with the fact that you are now safe in the cabin.

Step 1: TRUTH.   You *are* safe.

This *is* true. However, since you don't *know* you're safe, you could still die of that heart attack. So what good would your safety do you? None! It isn't enough to *be* safe. You must believe it.

The critical factor in my little story is time. As time marches on, you are going to survey your situation and ultimately come to the conclusion, *I believe I'm safe in this cabin.* This is *faith*.

Step 1: TRUTH.   You *are* safe.

Step 2: FAITH.   I *believe* I am safe.

This is not Christian faith; it's *cabin* faith — faith in the cabin and the cabin's ability to meet your need. It will take you who have what I call "feeler flesh" much longer to arrive at step 2 than it will others. You have a flesh pattern of believing that your feeler is usually telling it like it is. You often arrive at "truth" by trusting in your emotions; you make *them* the object of your faith. (Faith is a function of the mind; it means believing something, and it must have an object. It is never a feeling, but a belief upon which you take action. And it's a fatal mistake to *always* make feeler faith's object.)

Now that step 2 has arrived, you begin saying things like, "Oh, I'm so thankful! Without this cabin, I'd be dead!" But all the time you're *saying* how safe you are, you remain plastered to the wall. Can you see that even after arriving at step 2 you could still die of a heart attack *with your faith?* What good would your faith do you? None, because it is *faith without works*. Faith without appropriate action won't do you one whit of good. You might as well not have any faith at all (see James 2:17).

Knowing that you're now safe, why would you be acting as if you're *unsafe?* Because the intensity of your faith (in your mind) is about a two, whereas feeler is still demanding its way at level ten. Will is choosing to go along with feeler's assessment of the situation, even though will knows better. Feeler's recommendation is five times stronger than mind's at this point. Will is intimidated and chooses to go along with feeler's demands in an effort to relieve the pressure. But remember who's boss. Will *can* overrule feeler or mind or both simultaneously, *no matter how intensely* they apply pressure to sway his choice. Will is in charge.

Feeling Saved

This disparity between faith and feelings has a direct and important spiritual parallel. I've had many people come into my office during my years as a counselor and say to me, "I just can't get Jesus to save me. I try to get Him to come into me, but He just never has. I can't feel Him at all. I thought I did one time, but it went away." They want to *feel* saved. Typically, these are the "feeler folks." Unless they can feel something, they have difficulty accepting it as reality.

The Word of God never says, however, that anyone will *feel* saved. It says things like "Believe in the Lord Jesus Christ, and you shall *be* saved," not *feel* saved (Acts 16:31, emphasis added). As I lecture around the country, I take straw polls, asking the audience how many of them felt Christ enter into them when they were saved. The results (among charismatics and non-charismatics alike) are about fifty-fifty. God chooses to give a feeling to some folks, but He chooses not to give one to others, and I guess that falls under the heading of "His business." But even if He should give you a zingy feeling to boost you off the launching pad into the Christian life, it's only got about a ninety-day warranty. It's going to dissipate. It's got to at times, because the Lord has no interest in strengthening your fleshly pattern of being controlled by your emotions. "Without faith it is impossible to please Him" (Heb. 11:6).

God is committed to training you to walk in the Spirit by faith, and a critical part of that training is to teach you that you cannot trust your feeler, but you *can* trust Him. At times, He'll give you all the zingy feelings you can handle, but He will not permit you to build a tabernacle there. Sometimes it'll feel as though He's gone to Mars for a summer vacation. He will withdraw all experiential evidence of His presence to train you, indeed, to box you in and force you to walk by what you know rather than what you feel. But has He left you in those times? No. How could He do that? Your earthsuit would fall over and die if He left, because He *is* your life. Your job is to keep believing He has everything under control. It's just that He's allowed a testing time to come upon you. Don't be anxious about it (see Phil. 4:6). Keep operating by what you know.

Performance

With the passage of additional time in the Alaskan cabin, you will arrive at step 3, which the King James Version of the Bible calls "works." That means performance, activity, behavior. You've got to put some action to your faith if it's ever to benefit you. Mind is going to say, "That bear can't get into this cabin!

Here I am with sweaty palms, dry mouth, heart palpitations, and shaky knees. I'm going to have a heart attack if I don't get my act together! Get off this wall! Sit down on that floor and relax!"

Will is beginning to act on mind's suggestion instead of feeler's and is starting to slap feeler around a little. "Now, relax," you tell yourself, "shake it out. Breathe slowly and deeply. Close your eyes. Don't look at that bear. That'll just get my emotions all bent out of shape again. Plug your ears; don't listen to him. Unclench your teeth, and let your tongue unstick from the roof of your mouth. Now, imagine some relaxing scene in your mind like sitting in the sun out on the creek bank in the springtime. Relax!"

You are now choosing—forcing yourself—to "live like a safe man lives." You are bringing your behavior into line with the truth, according to your faith. The Bible calls this "walking in the light." You are choosing to go against feeler's recommendation because mind has gotten more information about the security of your situation. You might say your faith has increased as a result of becoming better acquainted with the object of your faith (cabin). Will has now determined that it would be the wise thing to overrule feeler's intense recommendation in favor of mind's weaker one. You have thus arrived at step 3.

Step 1: TRUTH.   You *are* safe.

Step 2: FAITH.   I *believe* I am safe.

Step 3: WORKS.   *Live* like a safe man lives.
                   Act like a safe man.

The Bossman Takes Over

As will forces all your members (except feeler) to relax on the floor and insists on exercising the authority that is his by God's edict, step 4 will evolve. We will label step 4 "Feelings."

Step 1: TRUTH.   You *are* safe.

Step 2: FAITH.   I *believe* I am safe.

Step 3: WORKS.   *Act* as though you are safe.

Step 4: FEELINGS. I finally begin to *feel* safer—
                   sort of.

Your feeler will gradually begin to respond because you have chosen to act the way safe people act. Notice that step 4 says "I finally begin to feel saf*er*—sort of." In other words, you can never get complete control over your emotions. True, you can exercise some control over them, but never total control. It is humanly impossible to do so. God has created us to be unable to control the emotions. As a saved person, you can control your mind and your will, but not your feelings. God's plan is for us to *believe* Him and choose to submit ourselves to His loving care and authority regardless of how we feel.

Jesus Could Not Control His Emotions

Jesus Christ could not control His emotions when He walked planet earth. Have you ever thought of that? He took on the form of a man and chose to acquire man's limitations (see Phil. 2:5-8). Consider the scene in the garden the night before the crucifixion. The Bible says that Christ's "sweat became like drops of blood" (Luke 22:44). Tell me, what were His emotions doing if His earthsuit was sweating blood? They were a fourteen. *Your* emotions have never been that high. "You have not yet resisted to the point of shedding blood in your striving against sin" (Heb. 12:4). That passage isn't speaking of Calvary, but of Gethsemane.

Let's say that you were there in the garden with Him and spoke to Him. "Excuse me, Sir, but it would appear that You have lost Your peace that You speak of so often. Have You?"

He'd answer, "Oh, no, I have great peace. But it's a peace that passes [human] understanding. The peace I have is knowing something. It's a function of the mind, not the emotions. It is knowing that My Father has everything under control. He and I discussed the events of tomorrow before I became a human being. As it approaches, I dread what is to come and have asked My Father if there isn't another way, but all I am getting is silence from Him."

Do you know how I know Christ got silence? Because if the Father had answered no and He'd persisted in asking (which He did), that would have constituted rebellion, and He would have been unable to be our Savior.

Silence is a very normal part of the victorious Christian life at times. When that happens, we must just forge ahead based on what we believe the Bible teaches His will to be for us, trusting that if our fine tuner is off, He will reveal it to us. I want His will for my life, and He wants His will for my life. If I'm seeking His will, it's His move if I'm a bit off the course He wants for me. I am to behave according to my understanding of His Word and ways, believing that He is leading me.

Christ would then continue to say of emotions, "Human beings often cannot understand the peace of which I speak, because the only peace they typically comprehend is a feeling. They want to *feel* peaceful. They will tell you that they have great peace of mind, but they don't. It's just that they feel good, so they set their minds on how good they feel. Let adverse circumstances arise, and they'll tell you they've lost their peace of mind. However, they never had peace of mind in the first place. It's simply that their feelers have gone off the Richter Scale, and now they're keeping their minds set on how bad they *feel*. It was *feel* peace instead of *mind* peace all the time."

How Satan Uses Feeler Flesh

Let's look at an example of how the Evil One will use a woman's stuck feeler to control her if he can. Let's make her thirty-two years old and married to a believer. Sharon, we'll call her, experienced considerable rejection from her dad. Her feeler was subsequently stuck on seven. She feels rejected by males at level seven on her very best days. Thus, she's got only three points of tolerance for rejection on her emotional Richter Scale, and with that she attempts to handle perceived rejection (whether it's actual or not).

On this particular day, she has planned a beautiful evening at home with her husband. Her idea is to surprise him, having farmed the kids out to Grandma. She has her best tablecloth and china out with all the trimmings. She's worked so hard, and now she has her nails painted and her prettiest dress on. It's going to be hamburger steaks for two by candlelight. Oh, how she hopes nothing will spoil this exciting evening!

Then Big Daddy comes home. "Surprise, surprise," she says "Tea for two, and the kids are over at Mom's! Just you and me and the candles."

He replies, "Oh, my soul! They called me from the church today, and they're one man short on the church bowling team. I told them I'd fill in."

"But, Honey—candles, china, perfume, nails."

To which he responds, "Sugar, you know how much I'd like to stay, but we're bowling against the Mormons tonight. This one's for *Jesus*. Just put my hamburger steak between some bread. I'm sorry, but I have to go." And out the door he goes, into his car and down the street.

The poor woman's brain processes this episode, and a print-out (perception) is generated: "Husband going bowling instead of staying here to party with me." Now an interpretation must be made by the computer analysts in Sharon's head (mind, emotions, sin, and the Holy Spirit). Sin comes on loud and strong, "I *believe* Earnest is rejecting me." Note that this is step 2, faith, from our hierarchy of steps that we developed in the story about the bear. When Sharon accepts sin's thought, feeler reacts (step 4, feelings), "I *feel* rejected two points worth."

We must remember, however, that our little wife has only three points of tolerance for feeling male rejection, so her feeler goes from seven to nine, not from one to three. Now, with the intensity of this high feeling to capitalize on, sin says to mind, (step 2, faith), "Well, since I *feel* such intense rejection, I really believe Earnest is rejecting me, and that's an eight!" Sharon swallows this line from sin. And once she accepts this thought, it's *her's*.

Feeler (step 4, feelings), triggered still higher by the process described in the rattlesnake story in Chapter 1, quickly tries to zoom up another three points. But wait a minute. Sharon's elevator can only go up one more floor, and then she'll be at ten. Thus, the intensity of the emotional strain becomes highly motivating. It's at this point that sin "assures" her that she has arrived at step 1, truth. Sin says, "It's *true*. Earnest has rejected me! Don't bother me with the facts. I *know* how I *feel*."

Do you see how the power of sin has taken a circumstance in this lady's life and, capitalizing on her unique version of the flesh, has deceived her into arriving at "truth" through her emotions? This dear lady may be quite logical in her thinking when it comes to following a recipe's instructions, but when it comes to interacting with other people, herself, or God, she makes her emotions the object of her faith and goes by what feeler says is truth. This whole process takes perhaps two or three seconds, and then she's under sin's control.

About two minutes later, however, here comes hubby's car back up the drive. He walks into the house, repentant over his mistake. It seems the Holy Spirit showed him he was making a mistake before he reached the stop sign at the end of the block, and he responded in obedience by returning with nary a bite taken from his hamburger steak. "I'm sorry, Honey," he says. "The Lord showed me how wrong I was to disappoint you after all your plans. Here, pop my burger into the microwave while I go change into something more comfortable for our party." And off he goes into the back bedroom.

Now her sound mind generates, "Wow, he didn't reject me! He's back. Oh, thank You, Lord, for answering my prayer." You see, mind has the capacity to change instantly. It has accepted as fact that whereas it formerly believed she was being rejected, it has now dismissed the thought. But how about feeler? It's still sitting on ten, and it's going to stay there for a while. In fact, since it was energized to try to go to twelve, it'll have to experience at least two and a half points of "cool down time" before she'll feel any relief at all.

Now, the devil isn't going to let this golden opportunity pass. Capitalizing on the wide "credibility gap" between the belief mind is attempting to embrace and the way she feels, sin is going to feed thoughts rapidly into her "sound mind" to try to take advantage of feeler's inability to respond quickly to truth. Sin will do his dirty work in accordance with this woman's flesh pattern. If she has "pity-party flesh," sin will serve up thoughts such as these to her mind: "As hard as I worked and planned for this evening to be special! And for him to treat me this way! Sure, he came back, but the louse left in the *first* place, didn't he! Does *he* ever plan anything nice for me? Oh, no, he's too busy worrying about how he can be the big Christian helper at the church! He always takes me for granted!" See how effective this would be, especially if it is laced through with truth and near-truth?

On the other hand, Sharon may have "beat-on-myself" flesh, and if so, sin will give her thoughts such as these, "I never do anything right. I try so hard to plan things well, and it seems like everything *always* turns out wrong for me. I'm so yukky! I just hate myself! If only I were different! I can't even compete with a bowling ball! I can't blame him for not wanting to stay home with a dullard like me."

You get the picture. The Evil One will serve up whatever sequence of thought patterns will best enable him to deceive the believer under the circumstances. The trick is that he must maintain a low profile to keep from being discovered, and the key is to serve up very "familiar" thoughts, thoughts that were very much a part of the "old man's" experience. Once Sharon embraces these thoughts, she is now sinning in her thought life (in that she has failed to refuse the thoughts).

The only step left in our hierarchy is step 3, works. Overt behavior will follow close on the heels of the inner buildup of frustration. This behavior will once again be a function of a person's unique version of the flesh. If the old patterns are for dumping hostility onto others, Big Daddy is going to get punched out as soon as he returns to the kitchen all showered and perfumed and with his new jump suit on. Hardly what he anticipated!

If Sharon has flesh patterns for dumping her hostility back on herself, on the other hand, he may walk into an awfully quiet kitchen. "What's the matter, Honey? I said I was sorry."

"Oh, it's nothing. I'm just a little tired tonight." And then the meal is taken in silence except for "Please pass the salt." She manages to say that she's had a hard day and wants to get a good night's rest before she departs for the bedroom with a "headache." He watches TV, wondering how the bowling match came out but afraid to phone anyone to ask.

You can never make the victorious Christian life a reality approaching it by the faith, feel, stronger faith, truth, actions sequence. God has prescribed one and only one way to consistent, moment-by-moment victory. And that way is the way of faith and obedience, never the way of the emotions. It is applying the Biblical steps in proper order: truth, faith, behavior, and feelings. If the feelings are reluctant to line up, ignore them. You can walk in complete victory without their lining up for as long as He wills it. You can make it work with only the first three. God will grant you the grace to enable you to do so. Just go for it. He'll take care of your feeler in His time after He has taught you to *walk in the Spirit by faith.*

Finally, the state of your emotions is never *the* criterion of whether you are walking in victory or not. Lining up on the Word of God by faith and obedience is the sole criterion you can trust.

Questions for Further Study

1. How important is it to feel the presence of God consistently in your life?

2. Do you believe the man in the cabin was being hypocritical as he began forcing himself to act safe when the bear was still at the door? Do you think it is hypocritical for a Christian to act contrary to his feelings if his feelings don't line up with God's Word? Give the reasoning for your answers.

3. As you reflect upon Jesus' prayers in the garden just before He was betrayed, what insights do you have that are applicable to your own prayers?

NINE

MAKING YOUR BEHAVIOR MATCH YOUR IDENTITY

A friend of mine who has made several trips to the Holy Land was telling me the other day how much different it was when he traveled with the tour guide he discovered on his fourth trip. This guide was Jewish, had been reared in Jerusalem, had studied Hebrew history in an Israeli university, and was also an enthusiastic Christian. He told me about some pretty exciting insights this guide had given him with regard to prophecy.

Personal experience is often invaluable if you are to serve as a guide to others. Accordingly, I'd like to relate briefly how the Holy Spirit took me through the experience that has "qualified" me to take pen in hand and to serve as a spiritual tour guide. I hope my experience will give you insight to help you appropriate your own victorious walk. We will also look at a step-by-step sequence of how to trust Christ to express His life through you as you face a particular task.

My Credentials (for Writing This Book)

Before coming to the end of my resources in attempting to live the Christian life, I depended on *my* ability. I saw all Christians as working *for* God. It was as if He needed my help. I never stopped to ask myself if He was that impotent. I just went along with the program of my church and "tried to do my best for God." Sound familiar?

I received my doctorate in counseling from Oklahoma State University and accepted an appointment as a psychology professor in the Oklahoma higher education system. I was very proud. *Dr.* Gillham! Hot dawg! "Lord, here I go to my new job," I prayed. "And my main goal is going to be to win souls for You in my new position. Man, what an influence I'll have for You — a born-again psychology professor on a university campus! You must admit You don't have many of those around!"

I have since envisioned the Lord's saying to Himself, "Well, there he goes again. Bless his heart. That boy means well. He thinks he's going to that campus to help Me, and I'm really not so hard up that I have to depend on a man. I could raise up a stone to do My work if I chose to. But I love that boy! He has a good heart. However, since My strength shows up best in weakness and Bill sees himself as *strong for Me*, I'm going to have to allow him to get weak. Then, in his weakness, he will turn to Me as his strength, his only strength."

So the Lord allowed a little "all things" to come into my life. I'm speaking of Romans 8:28, 29, where He says that all things are going to be used by Him to conform me to the image of His Son. Now, I don't mean to be "familiar" with the Lord, but I do think He has a fine sense of humor, and I enjoy picturing Him that way at times. So maybe some angels said to Him, "Do you want Gillham to get a full order of 'all things' or a half order?"

"I believe you'd better give him a full order," the Lord no doubt replied.

I want you to picture me lecturing to my new psychology classes. I'm well prepared, having generated and rehearsed my notes as best I could so as to make a good first impression. Oh, I so wanted to do well! But right in the middle of the lecture, it was as if my notes went cold. I couldn't figure out for the life of me what to say next. My lecture ground to halt, followed by fifteen seconds of awful silence while my face got as red as a beet. It was a terrible experience that I shall never forget.

I was desperately trying to salvage some pride (ugh!) out of the situation. "Lord!" I said. "I'm Your man on campus! Your saved 'sicoligy perfesser.' Your man-of-the-hour-with-power is in big trouble! My reputation, Lord! How will I work for You if I lose my reputation? Help!" And it was as if He'd gone to Jupiter.

I didn't keep a diary of those experiences, but their frequency was often enough to keep me paranoid about facing my classes. The circumstances varied in that sometimes they'd ask me a question I couldn't answer. It wasn't a question where I could say "I'll look it up and tell you later," but something like "What's Sigmund's last name again?" "When is your birthday?" Really tough ones! And there I'd go with the silence and red-face routine again.

I'd be strolling across the campus—I had a tweed sport coat and everything just like the "normal" professors—and here would come a cluster of kids. "Good morning, Dr. Gillham." Oh, I loved the sound of it! Here comes *Doctor* Gillham. And then the devil would tell me that I could know what they were *really* thinking about me: "There goes Delbert Dumb! What we don't need on this campus is another educated idiot." It nearly beat me to death. I didn't share my misery with anyone, not even Anabel. I was too ashamed.

I'd try binding the devil before I entered the classroom, and it was about as effective as screen doors on a submarine. I claimed the blood. I did everything I knew to do, and still I was a miserable failure as a psychology professor. Can you see God at work? He was allowing Satan to attack me in my area of "strength" to bring me to the end of myself, of my ability.

What's your source of pride, dear one? He hasn't got you reading this book as a time filler. You can choose to come to the end of yourself right now if you will. Or you can wait until the "all things" treatment forces you to come to grips with the flesh. How are you getting your needs met on this planet?

I don't know how long it took me to finally wake up and smell the coffee, but it was a long time. Finally, however, a pamphlet "somehow" came into my hands that spoke of my co-crucifixion with Christ. I couldn't understand it. I ultimately read it onto a cassette tape that I played over and over as I drove alone in my car. Finally I arrived at a point of very limited comprehension. I studied the Scripture references the writer cited and cross referenced them. I seemed to see a glimmer of hope. Christ, as my life, would teach the class through me.

I got on my knees in my bedroom and prayed, "Lord, I don't understand this, but the Bible says that the 'old me' died, the 'new me' was born, and Your desire is to express *Your* life through the new me. You want me to depend on You to teach those psychology classes through me, using my personality and my earthsuit to do it. Okay, Lord, I enter into that agreement. One thing I am convinced of: *I* can't teach the class. You do it."

Put Some Legs to the Commitment

Then I took a very important step, step 3 from the bear story: behavior. I got up off my knees and walked down the stairs *acting* as though Christ was going to do it through me. If I had waited on my knees until I "felt" Jesus take over and move me to the classroom and wiggle my lips for me, I'd still be there. We're not robots. *I* got up and *I* moved my legs in obedience, but I *believed* by faith that Christ was doing it through me be-cause the Bible says He *is my* life, my *only* life. But I *felt* like a hypocrite. Like the biggest phony in town! I did it anyway, how-ever, because I was desperate. I was at the end of *my* resources. I couldn't hack it anymore, and I knew it.

Thus, I began my new walk of *utter dependency*. I dared not depend on *my* university training, *my* skills as a communicator, *my* cleverness, *my* ability. I had depended on all those things before, and they had let me down like the *Titanic*. I wanted out, and I believed I had seen a Biblical crack in the door that would bail me out of this awful situation and glorify Christ if He pulled it off. I was going to let the Lord do it *all* through me. And it worked! Praise God, it worked, and it's still working! It's work-ing just as well for multitudes of Christians who have come to the end of themselves and claimed their true identity in Christ with Christ *as* life. Our brother Paul said it best, "For to me, to live is Christ" (Phil. 1:21).

"Lord," I prayed, "there are classes I must prepare for and lectures I must deliver. But with this new arrangement, I'm sure glad that I don't have to do either of them. You will do it all for me. You have *commanded* me to cast my burden upon You in Psalm 55:22. That's not an option, but an order! Okay, I'm casting this on You. You do it." And then *I set about acting as though He was doing it all through me.*

My lecture notes still looked the same — balloons with arrows zooming across the page, and so on. The pages didn't begin to fill up with automatic writing. If something like that had hap-pened, I'd have begun to "walk by sight," which would have created yet another problem that God would have had to help me overcome. I simply had to *believe* that He had taken over, that everything was now under His control and was His responsibility. I gave it my best. I applied all the knowledge of psychology I possessed. I tried to generate the best lecture notes I was capable of, but I gave Him the responsibility for it. If it turned out praiseworthy, to God be the glory. If it didn't, to God be the responsibility, and praise Him anyway! The monkey was on *His* back to produce, not on mine. Hallelujah! This is what He meant when He said His yoke is easy. What freedom! Not freedom to goof off, but freedom to see His power through me.

White Sands Proving Ground (Testing Time)

Here's an example of how it actually worked: I'm walking down the hall toward my Abnormal Psychology classroom. Do I *feel* confident that this is going to work? No! I feel insecure, just like always. Is there any guarantee I'll be successful? It all depends on your definition of success. If you're defining it as "perfect performance with perfect results," the answer is no. If you're defining it as "perfect *method*, trusting Christ as my life," the answer is yes.

What a relief! I began to sail along, class after class without a hitch. There was no hint of the old memory lapse problems — until one fateful day. Here it came, the test. I could detect it immediately, and I saw my options. I could choose the panic road, or I could choose the road of faith and obedience. I said, "Okay, Lord, here it is. It looks bad for the home team. I'm glad it's not my responsibility to pull it out. I'm blank! I'm sure glad You're on the hook. You can do whatever You want. If You want to let me look like a Delbert Dumb, go ahead. Let me get red as a beet. That's okay. I'll hate it, but that's Okay. That'll be Your problem, too." I gave Him permission to let the worst thing I could think of at the moment happen to me. The worst fear the devil could suggest. And He pulled me through. Praise the Lord, He pulled me through!

You say, "Bill, that's too simple. You have no comprehension of what kind of a pickle I'm in. My life makes your situation look like Ned in the first reader." I hear you, and you're right; I don't know what your situation is. But I can tell you this. Trusting Christ as my life has carried me through the experience of having a mentally retarded son. It has carried me through fathering four physically incomplete sons and agonizing and wishing that there were something I could do, even to exchanging places with them if it were possible. It carried me through speaking at my son's funeral. It has reduced my super-critical tongue, which was formerly being used to destroy my beautiful, faithful wife and my dear sons — while all the time I was striving to stop doing "the very thing I hated" — to a trickle. It liberated me from lusting after nearly anything in a skirt, whether in or out of church.

Oh, dear friend, God's grace *is* (not will be) sufficient for your situation. *He* wants to carry it all *for* you. Won't you give up and let Him live through you? You don't need to wait for one single thing to be added to who you already possess if you know Christ as Savior. Just celebrate a good funeral for the "old man," and then celebrate the birth of the new, victorious you who arose in Christ by *beginning to act like who you are.*

Testing times will come, but the one who is in charge of the "obstacle course" has designed it to motivate you to claim Him *as* your strength. He will not allow it to destroy you. The "course" is specifically designed to conform you to the image of your lovely older brother. Relax in it. Keep your mind on this. Our moment-by-moment battle is to fix in our minds that we *are* resting in heaven in Christ while simultaneously setting our minds to move through our daily tasks, believing that Christ is meeting them through us. *We work at resting while we rest at working.*

Making It Practical

We will now apply the four-step sequence of truth, faith, works, and emotions from the previous chapter to develop a technique for walking in the Spirit rather than "according to the flesh." I have a friend, Paul Burleson, who states, "Just as it is important for every Christian to know who he *is* in Christ, it is also important for him to know who he *was* prior to salvation if he is to understand 'walking according to the flesh.' " That's true, and if you check the areas where you seem to have the most difficulty walking in the Spirit, you'll discover it's in those areas where your emotions seem to be stuck. You've probably verbalized it as "My emotions shoot up to ten almost instantly." In all probability, however, this is a misperception. Your emotions *began* their journey up from a base of six or seven or even nine. It was but one short hop to the top for many of you.

We will take each step from the bear story illustration, recall how it applied to the bear and the cabin, and then make practical applications to the spiritual walk.

Step 1: Truth

The truth is: (1) the believer is identified with Christ in His death, burial, resurrection, and ascension to the Father's right hand. (2) Christ *is* now my life here on earth, and His will is to express His life through me. (3) I am resting *in* Him in His victory. The Bible states these truths in Romans 6, Colossians 3, and elsewhere. These verses *are* true, whether people accept them or not, because God said so. They are true of all who are born again. Thus:

Steps	Walking By Faith Steps	Bear Story Steps
Truth	All Christians are identified with Christ in His death, burial, resurrection, and ascension.	You *are* safe in the cabin.

You will recall that even though it was true that the man was safe in the cabin in the bear story, he could have died of a heart attack because he did not *know* he was safe. Similarly, there are millions of Christians who, due to a lack of understanding will die and go to heaven this year having never benefited from the truths of these verses. They are not "heaven verses" but "earth verses" to be appropriated *here*. They *are* true. There's an old saying: "What you don't know won't hurt you." That may apply in some cases, but in the Christian faith, what you don't know will destroy you.

Step 2: Faith

I wonder if you have enough faith to make these steps work. Let's run a quick test and see. Do you believe the Bible is the Word of God? You say, "Yes, I sure do." You just passed the test. You've got all the faith you need.

Many well-meaning Bible teachers will tell you that the reason you have no victory is that you need to get more faith. But if you want an exercise in futility, try to generate more faith by tomorrow morning. Talk about sending someone on a guilt trip! You don't need more faith. You need more knowledge of the object of your faith (see Appendix D).

Suppose you enter a church and observe the pews. You conclude, "I believe that pew will support my weight," and you sit down. Sure enough, it does. That's faith. It's not Christian faith; it's pew faith. Let's suppose, however, that the pew were to collapse. Did your faith let you down? No, your faith was sufficient. It was the *object* of your faith (the pew) that let you down. The pew wasn't worthy of the trust you placed in it.

God's love and trustworthiness, on the other hand, are always dependable. You must put your faith in *Him*, the beautiful object of your faith. You don't need great faith, but more understanding of the object of your faith.

Step 3: Works, Performance, Behavior

Remember, however, that the man in the cabin had faith, too. He believed he was safe, but he still could have died of a heart attack *with his faith*, because he failed to *act* like he believed it. Similarly, I have talked to people who tell me, "Oh, yes, the old truths of our crucifixion with Christ. I believe that. Why, I've known those truths for years. I did an extensive study on that and taught it to a Bible class." But stay around these people and watch them operate. Anyone with a half-ounce of spiritual discernment can detect that they are neither resting in the Lord nor allowing Christ to express His gentle, loving life through them to others.

It isn't enough to just "have faith." You've got to add something to your faith if you would walk in the Spirit. You've got to act as if you have faith. Remember at the beginning of the chapter how I had to get off my knees and act as though Christ is living through me? Well, so do you. You must step out on your faith.

Here is the step where most Christians miss the mark. The flesh wants to skip over step 3 and move directly to step 4, feelings. The flesh loves to *feel* something happen as "proof" that things are now different, that "it has worked." The flesh always "seeks for a sign" so it can hang its hat on the sign instead of on the Word of God. *It wants to use the sign as the object of its faith rather than the Word that God has spoken.* Many believers walk by this motto: "A sign a day proves the devil's away."

This is no longer *your* way, however, it's the way of your flesh. The way of the Spirit is now your way. "However, you are not in the flesh but in the Spirit" (Rom. 8:9). But even though it is no longer your way, it certainly *is* your "old ways," and indwelling sin will continually bug you with first-person-singular-pronoun logic that his way is the true way (see Appendix E).

Success by Whose Definition?

The dictionary defines failure as "not succeeding" and customarily refers to a performance task. Christians have been deceived into believing that we should be able to design and build an improved computer, be a perfect mother with perfect kids, or install a new electrical outlet in the kitchen for the wife's food blender, as "I can do all things through Him" (Phil. 4:13). Well-meaning disciplers cite this verse to struggling believers as "proof" that they should be able to handle *any* performance task successfully. This is not true. Neither this passage nor the rest of Scripture teaches that.

Instead, this oft-quoted passage (Phil. 4:11-13) refers to our being able to maintain a *stability of mind* as we experience all circumstances, resting in Christ as we do so. This is the "secret" spoken of in verse 12: "I know how to get along with humble means, and I also know how to live in prosperity; in any and every circumstance I have learned the secret of being filled and going hungry, both of having abundance and suffering need." You see, it never implies the perfect results the flesh craves. It implies perfect *method*, resting in the Lord and His sufficiency to supply all my need. We can praise the Lord whether we're eating peanut butter or steak. He's got everything under control.

A Simple Illustration

We'll use a simple performance task to illustrate the Biblical method of how to "turn it over to the Lord." There is this woman whose husband likes his eggs cooked over easy for breakfast. If she accidentally breaks a yolk, he has been known to storm away from the table and leave for work without any breakfast, making her feel terribly guilty. He's a real doll.

Each day she carries the same burden at 6:45 A.M. — eggs to be cooked. We'll construct a grid to help us organize the events of her experience so we can apply Biblical methodology in analyzing whether she is walking in the Spirit or walking according to the flesh in doing this job.

**The
Burden**
Eggs to
be cooked

Now, how will she solve the problem? She will use the method found in the "Self-Help" section of the local psychotherapy clinic library. Her method is "I must do this myself." Her thinking is, *I can't bother the Lord with such trivial matters as egg-cooking. After all, I'm perfectly capable of doing this myself. God expects me to carry my end.*

Her method, in other words, is *independence*. God despises independence. He loves dependence. He desires that believers depend upon Him and His ability to supply all their needs, remember? Independence says, "I can supply my own needs. In fact, *I am my own supply.* I don't need You, God, except for the things I can't do alone, such as take myself to heaven. So go help the weaker ones, Lord, who, unlike me, are not able to help themselves. Thank You, God, for making me so strong" (see Appendix F).

| **The
Burden** | **Method
Used** |
|---|---|
| Eggs to
be cooked | Do it
myself |

Next step: "Now, Lord, I really would like perfect eggs to be cooked this morning. I'm going to do the best I can, but You know, Lord, sometimes they break in spite of all I can do. I would appreciate it if You'd just take up the slack and help me a bit if the eggs are in danger of breaking." Under this method, you see, the better she can do things alone, the less she needs to depend on the Lord and His strength. So we add this to the grid.

The Burden	Method Used	Desired Results
Eggs to be cooked	Do it myself	Unbroken yolks

Lo and behold, they turn out perfect this morning. Two prettier eggs she's never laid eyes on. It looks like this day is starting off right. We'll add this to the grid.

The Burden	Method Used	Desired Results	Actual Results
Eggs to be cooked	Do it myself	Unbroken yolks	Unbroken yolks

How does the flesh react? "Success! Look at those eggs! Perfect! I sure hope Joe responds to me this morning and gives me some recognition for all I do for him."

The flesh, having been programmed through years of living in the jungle warfare of planet earth, striving to get needs met through worldly methodology, always looks to tangible results to evaluate success and failure. If the results are perfect, the flesh says "success"; if the results are poor, the flesh says "failure." Also, the flesh expects a return on its investment of "service rendered." I call it "fish hook love," because it always has a catch to it: "I've done something nice for you. Now it's your turn to do something nice for me."

The Burden	Method Used	Desired Results	Actual Results	Flesh's Evaluation
Eggs to be cooked	Do it myself	Unbroken yolks	Unbroken yolks	Success

The Lord, however, gives this woman an F on her performance. "Lord, how can You do that? Just look at those eggs. They're perfect! Even my husband likes them," she might respond. "And everyone at church knows he has higher standards than You. Can't You give me at least a B or maybe B– ? I tried so hard to be pleasing for You."

Let's imagine that the Lord came down to converse with her in the same manner He did with Job. The Lord might say, "Now, my dear, I agree that the eggs look delightful. They are about as good as any wife could be expected to do. However, I'm not looking at the *eggs* to score you. I scored you F before you ever cracked the shells! You see, I score you on your method, *not* on your results. Your method was independence, self-sufficiency. That's the way of the world, the way of the flesh. And as for giving you a B or a B− grade, I always score people pass-fail, for your method is always either right or wrong. It is either trusting in the finished work of Christ at Calvary or trusting in flesh-proven techniques."

The one criterion by which we will be graded is whether our work is composed of the same substance as the foundation, which is Christ. The life of the vine is the same life that's in the branches. The work will be tested by fire to determine whether it was accomplished with vine life or flesh. It's *how* we build, not *what* we build. Read 1 Corinthians 3:11-15 carefully, slowly. Your work is either gold, silver, and precious stones or wood, hay, and stubble. That's pass-fail.

God said to Abraham, "Take now your son, your *only* son . . . and offer him . . . as a burnt offering" (Gen. 22:2, emphasis added). But wait a minute. Abraham had two boys, Isaac and Ishmael, didn't he? No. God was speaking of Isaac, the "son of promise," and His attitude was, "Abraham, you have only one son that I recognize. That other son is the result of your, Sarah's, and Hagar's fleshly action as you were trying to 'help Me' bring about My promise." Only God's work will be acknowledged by God at the Judgment Seat of Christ. That is precisely why even though some believers will see their entire earthly performance consumed by the fire, they, themselves, will be saved. Salvation, after all, is a work of God, not of the flesh, and that's the reason it will pass safely through the fire (1 Cor. 3:15; see also Appendix G).

With that understanding, we can see that our grid will now look like this:

The Burden	Method Used	Desired Results	Actual Results	Flesh's Evaluation	God's Evaluation
Eggs to be cooked	Do it myself	Unbroken yolks	Unbroken yolks	Success	Failure

Finally, our housewife recognizes that something is drastically wrong with her approach as she experiences a roller coaster Christian life. The Holy Spirit speaks to her through His Word, a pamphlet, a tape, a book, or whatever, and the lights turn on. She sees that she is to let the Lord live His life through her, even to cook eggs. What a relief! Praise the Lord! He's taken the burden off her. He desires to carry it all. So now we'll construct a new grid based on her new discovery.

The Burden	Method Used	Desired Results	Actual Results	Flesh's Evaluation	God's Evaluation
Eggs to be cooked	*Trust Christ through me*	Unbroken yolks	Unbroken yolks	Success	Success

Notice that the burden is still the same, eggs to be cooked, but look at the method. She's chosen to turn the burden over to the Lord. She's going to choose against her unique version of the flesh (which is self-reliance) and become dependent. She says, "Lord, I'm going to act as though You are cooking these eggs through me, because the Word says You are my life." The desired results are still the same, unbroken yolks. And look at the actual results, unbroken yolks!

Even though God now approves of the wife's egg cooking, however, He's also saying, "Yes, I'm pleased, but we have a major problem here. You are swallowing the flesh's definition of success. You're looking at the eggs, and because they're perfect, you believe Jesus cooked them through you. You are looking at the results for 'proof' that Christ really *is* your life. You're making the *results* the object of your faith instead of My Word. You are walking by sight, not by faith.

"Now, I'm going to let you practice Christ as life with pretty eggs for a while to get you started off the launch pad, but ultimately I'm going to have to break you from walking by sight."

We will now construct our third and final grid, which will illustrate how the Lord will accomplish this goal through the use of His "obstacle course." This dear Christian lady deeply desires to walk in victorious obedience, and the Lord is going to reveal His provision for accomplishing exactly that.

The Burden	Method Used	Desired Results	Actual Results	Flesh's Evaluation	God's Evaluation
Eggs to be cooked	Trust Christ through me	Unbroken yolks	Broken yolks	*Failure*	Success

Here she is three weeks later, still trusting the Lord to cook the eggs through her. She's built up a pretty good confidence in His ability to do it through her by this point. She is being trained to abandon all confidence in self and self's ability to meet her needs.

On this eventful day that God has selected to teach her not to walk by sight, she says, "Okay, Lord, let's have two more perfect eggs. How I wish I could have learned this lesson years ago. I'm going to let You cook them through me. Okay, I believe that's enough time on that side, now let's turn them over nice and easy." But shock, horror! Look at the results! Broken yolks! What went wrong?

Notice how indwelling sin is going to take advantage of the situation. Sin says, "I blew it! I thought I had learned how to turn it over to the Lord, but I guess I haven't. Somehow *I* took over and ruined the eggs. The horrible thing about it is that I don't know exactly where I took the task back on myself, so how can I ever be secure that Jesus is living through me? I used all the faith I had. I'll never really *know* He's living through me. I guess I'll have to back off until I get some assurance that He *really is* living through me again before I can ever believe it's true. I sure wouldn't want to be a hypocrite."

The Lord says, "Oh, you didn't take over and break the yolks. I let them break to teach you not to walk by sight. I want you to just believe My Word. I said Christ *is* your life. *Your job is to do the very best you can, trusting that I'm doing it through you, and leave the results to Me.* If it turns out well, praise Me; if it doesn't, praise Me anyway, and let Me handle any problems that are created as a result. Your job is to concentrate on your *method*—dependency."

Thus, our task is to strive for excellence while at the same time trusting that Christ is living through us. The results are then *His* results, and we will praise Him in them.

In no way can we "put God in a box" and approach Christian victory by a cookbook-type manual. But when you're in the fourth grade and having trouble with your math, it's sometimes very helpful to sit down with a sixth grader and review the steps he's learned to solve his problems. (You will note I don't claim to have a Ph.D. in Christian living.)

Let me summarize what we have learned thus far in the book:

FACTS:
- When Christ died, you died as an "old man."
- When Christ arose, you were born as a "new man."
- Christ is now the *only* life you have. Any other technique you employ for living is "death."
- Christ is now resting in heaven and so are you in Him.
- You have the same rights Jesus had when He left heaven and came to earth—none. You are a "living sacrifice." You are to "seek God first" and He will supply all your needs.

FAITH:
- You must believe the above based on revelation by the Holy Spirit to you from God's Word.

WORKS:
- Moment by moment, by faith, you are to act as though Christ is expressing His agape life through you to accomplish His will.
- You are to apply all diligence to the task.
- You are to study God's Word so the Holy Spirit can train you to discern good and evil, that you might not prostitute the life of Christ by living for self while claiming it to be the life of Christ through you.
- You are to rest in your mind that your method (faith and obedience) is correct.
- You are to rest in your mind that the results are Christ's results through you, and you are to praise Him whether "successful" or not.
- You are to recognize that your emotions are not your primary barometer of truth. God's Word is.

God's Acceptance Is Not God's Approval.

God accepts people on a pass-fail basis, as we've seen. His method is never performance-based, but Jesus-based. However, God's *approval* must be *earned*, and it definitely *is* performance-based. But the deception the enemy has propagated is that God's approval ("Well done, good and faithful servant") is scored on a curve, with Jesus establishing the top score. Not so! His scale for approval is scored the same as His scale for acceptance, pass-fail. When your earthly works are judged, if you have permitted Christ to express His life of love, obedience, and servanthood through you, you will hear, "Well done, good and faithful slave; you were faithful with a few things, I will put you in charge of many things" (Matt. 25:21).

Consider, however, a fictitious seminary professor who sees himself as helping God train men and women for service. Last semester he worked sixty hours per week, but he was saddened by his students' overall grade point average (GPA) of 2.1 on a 4 point scale. Burdened by the thought that they would head out into the fields inadequately prepared and that his commitment was limited to only sixty hours per week, he vowed before the Lord that he would increase his dedication.

He summarily informed his wife that he could no longer spend Sunday afternoons with the family; that God had called for greater dedication, and he'd have to spend his weekends at the office. He told his kids that he could no longer attend their recitals, ballgames, and so on because God's work comes first, and surely they wouldn't be so carnal as to want him to skip studying to attend their recitals.

This dear, well-meaning man abdicated his responsibilities as husband and father, ignoring God's *direct* commands, and never took his wife out or had time simply to be her friend (but was *always* on call night or day to his students) because he was driven by false guilt.

Even though he was losing his relationship with those nearest and dearest to him, his flesh was "comforted" by sin's telling him that he was in God's will now and earning "Well done" because the class GPA had risen to 2.85. He didn't *feel* as guilty as he did the previous semester, now that he was working a ninety hour week. He could accept himself better now.

Do you see, discerning Christian, that this dear man *already had* his reward? His results (increased GPA) were admirable; his method was the flesh. These works will be burned at the Judgment Seat of Christ. Thus, we complete step 3.

Steps	Walking By Faith Steps	Bear Story Steps
Truth	All Christians are identified with Christ in His death, burial, resurrection, and ascension.	You *are* safe in the cabin.
Faith	I believe the Bible (that I am identified with Christ).	I *believe* I'm safe.
Works	*Live as if it's all true in me.—Act* as though it is.	*Live* as a safe person lives. *Act* safe.

Step 4: Feelings

As I continue to walk by faith and obedience, setting my mind on the reality of how things are rather than on how I *feel* or on "circumstantial evidence" that belies God's Word, God will begin to bring my feeler's "stuck threshold" more into line. I'll be transformed by the renewing of my mind (Rom. 12:2). Thus, we complete the final step.

Feelings	I finally begin to *feel* more as if it's all true in me—*sort of.*	Same as left.

Notice I said "sort of." God is never going to bring your feeler *totally* into subjection so long as you remain in your earthsuit. He has deliberately designed it to vacillate so as to force you to walk by faith, not by feel, if you would experience the "peace that passes understanding." Remember, that peace is not a feeling, but a *knowing*—knowing that the Father has everything under control; that you are in Christ, seated in heaven, resting; and that He is in you now, living. Bow before Him right now. Praise Him for dreaming up such a fantastically innovative, glorious, gracious plan whereby you and I can face *anything* this world can throw at us, not due to *our* ability but to His ability through us.

Questions for Further Study

1. This chapter discusses the need to "put some legs" to your commitment. Has there been a time when you found yourself in a similar position as Bill in his psych classes? As you reflect on that time, what added insights do you gain looking at it again?

2. Do you get the idea that everything went great after Bill began to trust the Lord and walk in the Spirit? How do you account for your answer?

3. How would you "cook an egg sunny side up"?

TEN

"LEFTLY" DIVIDING THE WORD OF TRUTH

Maybe you're saying, "Bill, I see what you're teaching about the sin nature's being dead and how we now battle against the *power* of sin and the flesh. You just teach it a little differently from me. I call the power of sin the sin nature. It's a little different, but I believe we're both saying the same thing. It's just semantics."

I've had Bible teachers say that to me, but it's not correct. They and I are poles apart in our teaching. If they're right, I'm battling against *myself*. I'm fighting a *civil* war. If I'm right, on the other hand, I'm collaborating with the Holy Spirit to fight against sin. It's God and me against *him*. It's two against one and I can win! I'm "more than a conqueror through Him" (see Rom. 8:37).

The Bible can be interpreted as saying that salvation, security, sanctification, and all the rest of God's blessings must be *earned* through performance. But it can also be interpreted that these are *bestowed* upon the believer solely by grace through faith in the finished work of Christ.

Discerning the correct interpretation is critical to consistent victory over your version of the flesh. Does this mean I'm going to resolve theological issues that the world's greatest intellects have struggled to understand? Do I claim I can show you the "right" way? Well, I don't claim to have the market cornered on truth, but I do have an opinion. Whatever truth I have is purely by the grace of God, as is the case with anyone. I believe "rightly dividing the Word of truth" on all the attainable plateaus for the new creation in Christ is critical to consistent victory, and I have an opinion on how to go about understanding it that I believe is Biblical or I would abandon it.

One Spirit

Webster defines *enigma* as "a perplexing or baffling matter." This book interprets the Bible as teaching that no human being has two spiritual natures. Lost folks have one; saved folks have one. The Bible teaches that all people are spiritual creatures who temporarily dwell in earthsuits, not physical creatures who have spirits. There's a *big* difference in those two views. Our eternal identity is spiritual, not physical. This is true for both the saved *and* the lost. "Therefore . . . we recognize no man according to the flesh" (2 Cor. 5:16*a*). With this in mind, let's compare a Christian with an unbeliever as follows:

Variable	Unregenerate man	Regenerate man
spirit	dead	alive
nature	satanic	godly
family tree	son of Satan	son of God
condition	under condemnation	under grace
sins against God	guilty	forgiven
future	certain disaster	certain bliss and purpose
Jesus as ruler	rejected Him	submitted to Him
truth	rejected it	accepted it
mind	darkened, veiled	veil removed
will	rebellious to God	delights in God
affections	for things of world	for things above
Jesus	avoids Him	longs for Him
center of life	self	Christ
source	self	Christ

The above list is only partial, but one can readily see that it describes two polarized identities. We can condense each column into one summary label as follows:

1. Unregenerate man has a sin nature, meaning that he has a deep-seated *desire* to avoid Jesus' authority over him. He is committed to ruling his own life and destiny. *He* is his god.

2. Regenerate man is a "partaker of the divine nature." He has a deep-seated *desire* to submit to Jesus' authority over him. He is committed to submitting his life and destiny to Jesus. Jesus is *his* God, and he is delighted with the arrangement, even though he experiences some very difficult times on earth.

Now, here's the rub. We can find verses in the Bible that appear to teach that Christians have two natures, not one. How can we deal with that? Furthermore, there are other apparent contradictions in the Word, although we know the Word is totally true. For example, how about the verses that teach you have to be baptized to be saved versus those that teach you don't? And how about those that teach that a saved person can become unsaved versus those that teach he can't? What do we do with these? Which is the right position to take?

As I took this enigma to the Lord, studying His Word and striving to remain open to His Spirit, digesting the truth and discarding the error (including that in my own denomination's teaching) by His gracious revelation, I have some things to offer to you that I believe are from the Holy Spirit.

Two Roads

The Lord showed me that the Christian life is like a road upon which I travel and upon which I encounter a series of forks, each of which demands that I turn either to the right or to the left (see Figure 10.1). Choosing the correct fork may or may not be accompanied by feelings of euphoria, but the feeling (or its absence) must never become the object of my faith.

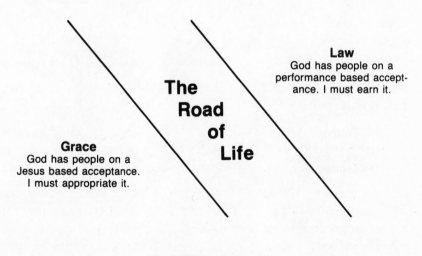

Law
God has people on a performance based acceptance. I must earn it.

The Road of Life

Grace
God has people on a Jesus based acceptance. I must appropriate it.

Figure 10.1

A right turn on this road leads to an area I'll label "Law." This stands for the concept that God has people on a performance-based acceptance; the more nearly our performance measures up to God's Law, the better He accepts us. Conversely, if we fail from time to time, His smile fades to a frown of rejection. The epitome of this condition would be to incur His ultimate rejection, eternity in hell.

Taking a left turn on this road, however, leads to "Grace," God's unmerited favor poured out upon undeserving humanity through Jesus Christ. After salvation, my motivation from this perspective is *not based on guilt over my failures*, but rather I am motivated *by love for Christ* to offer myself to Him, to let Him express His life through my personality and earthsuit to a hurting world. I believe correctly understanding the Word requires *separating law from grace*. Thus, a left turn is the right turn to take on this road, and hence the title of this chapter.

Salvation

Once upon a time, I traveled this road and encountered the very first fork in the way. I'll label this fork "Salvation" (see Figure 10.2).

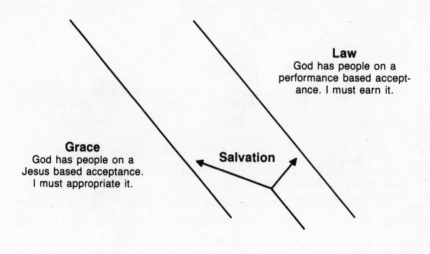

Law
God has people on a performance based acceptance. I must earn it.

Grace
God has people on a Jesus based acceptance. I must appropriate it.

Salvation

Figure 10.2

As the Holy Spirit was dealing with me, a group of people approached me with a tract containing "fifteen verses," that used the Bible to "prove" I'd best turn right toward law if I hoped to make it to God. But then there was a second group who approached me with a tract containing "fifteen verses" that Jesus had already paid it all and that I must simply accept His forgiveness by faith; that His death on the Cross had made my access to God a matter of pure grace, **G**od's **R**iches **A**t **C**hrist's **E**xpense. I chose the left-turn option and much to my delight, I have discovered through the Word and my experience that I now have the Holy Spirit of Christ Himself indwelling me. I am saved.

Baptism

Before long, I found myself at a second fork in this road, the fork of baptism (see Figure 10.3).

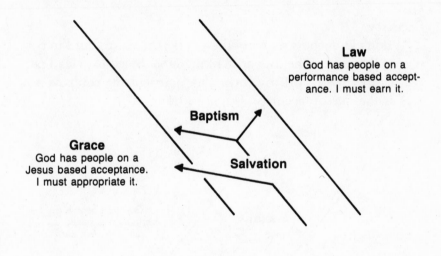

Figure 10.3

Another group of well-meaning folks approached me with a tract they'd developed containing "fifteen verses" to "prove" that unless I got baptized (and the message was urgently pressed upon me lest I die and miss my opportunity), I could not be saved. These folks were sincerely convinced that they were "rightly dividing the Word of Truth." But there came a second group of folks having a tract with "fifteen verses" showing me that baptism was but a pantomime depicting my death, burial, and resurrection with Christ, my public testimony to what had happened to me at salvation. They explained that baptism was a picture of God's grace. I chose to turn left at this fork also, believing it to be the rightly divided grace position rather than the law position.

I have received reinforcement from the Word, as well as from the indwelling Holy Spirit, that this was the correct way. For example, Paul said to the Corinthians in 1 Corinthians 1:14, 17, "I thank God that I baptized none of you. For Christ *did not send me to baptize*, but to preach the *gospel*" (emphasis added). Therefore, the pro-baptism group would have to declare Paul misguided in this verse, as he didn't include baptism in the gospel.

Security

I don't know how many of these forks there are, but I'm convinced that one of the functions of the Holy Spirit is to lead people up this road, fork by fork. One particularly controversial fork is the one of "security" (Figure 10.4).

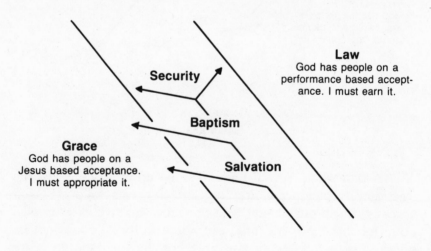

Figure 10.4

Well-meaning brothers and sisters in Christ will approach with a tract that quotes "fifteen verses" "proving" that I have to keep holding onto Jesus lest I slip and fall away into hell. Their position is that it is my job to keep myself saved through performance, and I've got to keep holding on (sometimes with oil-slick hands, it seems). In other words, I must perform to retain what I couldn't perform to acquire in the first place.

Then another group armed with a tract quoting "fifteen verses" takes the position that my security lies in the fact that Jesus holds *me*, not vice versa. They show me verses such as "No man can take [you] out of My hand" (John 10:28) and "I will never desert you, nor will I ever forsake you" (Heb. 13:5). By exercising spiritual discernment, I saw this position as adhering closer to the truth of God's grace and I turned left. As I have walked in this position over the years, the Holy Spirit has again and again reinforced the truth of it to my inner man.

Sanctification

There is one additional major fork in the road I wish to discuss, the fork about which the Lord has raised up this book. It's the fork of "sanctification" (see Figure 10.5).

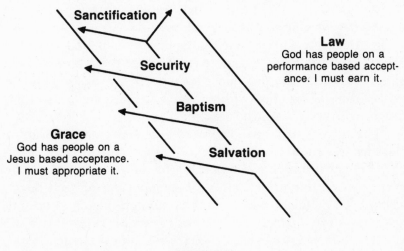

Figure 10.5

Are Christians a truly holy people, or are we trying to *become* a holy people? This fork represents our opportunity to accept or reject the death of the "old man." Groups of well-meaning Bible teachers approach with a tract of "fifteen verses" "proving" that to attain holiness, I must *stop* smoking, *stop* lying, *stop* cheating on my tax return, *begin* praying more, *begin* Bible memorization, *begin* witnessing, and so on. Through this process, we're told, I will become holier. It's *performance-based holiness*. It's law. God has some pretty strong things to say to us about avoiding that approach to holiness. "Hey, El Stupido! Having begun this process by the Spirit, are *you* now going to take over and complete it on flesh power?" (Gal. 3:3, loose paraphrase).

Then there are others who have discerned that the "mystery" of the gospel that liberates one to live a *consistent*, obedient life is found by turning left at this fork. I must believe at face value all the verses that document my new identity in Christ, that say I am literally a new person *now*. It is from *this* posture that I can begin to lay aside my old ways (smoking, lying, cheating) and put on the new (prayer, Bible memorization, witnessing, etc.).

It's not that I cease to have one identity and begin to have another as a gradual process. My old identity *terminated* at the Cross in Christ (see Gal. 2:20), and my new one *was created* (past tense) in godliness in Him at His resurrection (see 2 Cor. 5:21). I can become a mature example of who I already am. As an oak sapling grows, it doesn't get "oakier." Oak is oak. It simply *matures into* what it is, a full-grown oak tree.

It's the same with us. We *are* the holy sons of God. We don't get holier, more accepted, more justified, or more forgiven. We simply experientially "life out" who and what we already are. It's not a "from-to" situation with us. We *are* a holy people. Now let's get on with *acting* like who we are.

The tragedy is that most evangelicals have turned right at this fork and are beating their heads against a brick wall, striving to get holier through performance. One of the patriarchs of the faith who no doubt dedicated a major portion of each day to striving for holiness asked that the epitaph on his tombstone refer to him as a poor, wretched, worthless worm. And this was from one of the all-time champions of the faith. I just read today that one of the most intelligent, well-respected seminary professors in the land states that he completely identifies with that posture. What incentive to growth does that leave us plain folks in the pew? It's enough to make a person give up even trying, and that's exactly what I see in so many Christians. It is breaking God's heart.

The Key

We might want to ask at this point, "Well, Lord, why did You put all these forks in Your Word? It seems it would have been good to eliminate the opportunity for people to err by misinterpreting Your Word. Why did You do this? Why not sixty-six books clearly spelling it out in black and white?" And this is what I believe He has shown me in response to my seeking.

The devil is a liar; God is truth. That's a polarity. If I don't believe God, I lump Him in with His archenemy and imply that He, too, is a liar.

I believe every word in the Bible is inspired and absolutely true. It breaks my heart to hear a Christian leader state that in his "wisdom" he has come to "understand" that Jonah wasn't a literal man swallowed by a literal fish, or something like that. What a grief to the heart of God! (C. S. Lewis has an excellent treatment of the critical-historical view of Biblical interpretation and its devastating results in chapter 27 of *The Screwtape Letters*). I am delighted to be counted with the simple-minded who just believe what God says.

In giving me the opportunity to either believe or disbelieve, however, God has made Himself so vulnerable as to structure even His Holy Word so that the devil can use *even that* to deceive me. That's the way he tempted Jesus in the wilderness. He quoted Scripture to "prove" his point. He quoted it perfectly, but he misconstrued God's meaning. Jesus countered him by quoting opposite excerpts from God's Word that correctly interpreted God's will. Satan will try the same with you if he can. He seeks to malign God's integrity in your thoughts and deceive you.

The focal issue of all eternity is Christ on the Cross. Everything prior to that blessed event points to it; everything after it points back at it. It will always be so. Our God has scars in His hands that we will see daily throughout eternity.

Jesus Christ volunteered for the Cross to demonstrate one

attribute of God and one only. He did not hang there to demonstrate His omnipotence or omnipresence or any of His other characteristics. Christ on the Cross demonstrated God's limitless grace, His loving, forgiving grace.

Therefore, where law appears to conflict with grace in Biblical interpretation, fix your eyes on Jesus Christ on that Cross to "rightly divide" the passage. Put on *Son*-glasses, and filter every interpretation of the Word through Him there. The Holy Spirit will always point me toward grace, always. He will point the unbeliever to law to bring him to salvation, but He will never point the *believer* to law.

"The Power of Sin Is the Law" (1 Cor. 15:56)

"Realizing the fact that law is not made for a righteous man [and new creatures *are* righteous], but for those who are: lawless and rebellious, for the ungodly and sinners [remember, we are saints who sin], for the unholy and profane, for those who kill their fathers or mothers, for murderers and immoral men and homosexuals and kidnappers and liars and perjurers, and whatever else is contrary to sound teaching" (1 Tim. 1:9, 10).

The law is not for you if you're a new creation; it was used by the Lord to convict you of your hopeless state and thus motivate you to accept Jesus Christ as your Savior. Now that the law has served its purpose *for you*, you are no longer under it. But if you choose to stay under it and approach the Christian walk with the law attitude of "I must, I ought, I have to" instead of "I am new, I delight to do God's will, I love Him, His ways are good," you are laboring under law; you have not "entered into God's rest," and it's just a matter of time until you burn out.

"The *power* of sin is the law" (1 Cor. 15:56, emphasis added). *Law is the "gasoline" that fuels sin's engine.* That explains why we sometimes see a pastor who hammers away with law teaching run off with the church secretary. The power of sin in him "fed itself" on the man's teaching and destroyed his ministry with it. *You give the power of sin a law to work with and it will eventually beat you, because God's provision for the believer is grace, not law.*

Jesus satisfied the law for all who will appropriate His grace. Appropriate His finished work for you and you pull the teeth from the power of sin. You drain sin's gas tank! Tragically, many disciplers' major tool for trying to motivate a believer to grow is law. But God's plan is for us to learn who we now are and how to appropriate grace for victory in each day's circumstances, so Christ gets the glory. "Thanks be to God, who gives [that's grace] us the victory through our Lord Jesus Christ" (1 Cor. 15:57).

Always, Always Look to God's Grace

Thus, I believe that God has shown me, "Always turn left, Bill, and you'll be right. But if you ever turn right, you'll be left." Truly, any time a person takes a turn toward law, seeing himself on a performance-based acceptance with God, God will allow the individual to travel that wrong road until he hits a brick wall. He'll allow the devil to punch the "hold" button on the person's telephone and just let him sit there and blink. That person will never go on with God until he turns around and goes back to the fork where he made the wrong turn. I care not whether the fork represents a law position on baptism, eternal security, forgiveness, acceptance, righteousness, holiness, justification or anything else. You turn right and you'll be left. You'll wear out trying to measure up to law, and you'll crash sooner or later. Tragically, the dear people who turn right at the salvation fork will be eternally left. You cannot *earn* God's acceptance.

As C. S. Lewis said in *Mere Christianity*, "If, somewhere upon the road of life, you discover you have taken a wrong turn, the quickest way forward is to turn around and go back. Or, if somewhere along life's road you find yourself traveling with a group which has taken a wrong turn, the first man to turn around and go back is the most progressive."

I realize someone may use verses to "prove" that the Christian's old sin nature didn't die in Christ. *But he must arrive at that conclusion by turning right.* He must adopt the posture that a born-again person *attains* holiness through performance. The Word says, however, "The flesh [not the old man] sets its desire against the Spirit, and the Spirit against the flesh" (Gal. 5:17). It's not our old sin nature we struggle with. It's the *power of sin* working through the old, worldly ways. You will never get good, solid victory in this battle we all experience until you see by His Word and *appropriate* the truth that the old man literally died in Christ. It's not positional, it's literal. *Dead men tell no tales.* Those "tales" you experience moment by moment are being offered up to your mind by the deceiver of the brethren through your flesh.

Questions for Further Study

1. Why do you believe God's Word contains seemingly contradictory statements?

2. What is the primary key to correctly understanding and interpreting God's Word?

3. Perhaps you sense that you have made a turn toward law on the road of life. If so, what do you need to do?

4. If you believe that up to this time you have turned toward grace, what can you do to avoid taking any wrong turns toward law?

ELEVEN

IS GOD TRYING
TO TELL YOU
SOMETHING?

The pastor slumped in the chair across from my desk, his face giving silent witness to the turmoil within. He'd been very successful, having ascended to the position of heir-apparent of his denomination's highest state office.

Then the young divorcee came to him for counseling. In his zeal to help her, he became emotionally involved, and they eventually fell into sin. Their secret was exposed, and the pastor was dismissed in disgrace. Dashed were his dreams of denominational honors and esteem. Dashed were the long years of labor as he'd climbed the ladder through the tiny churches to the large city church. There he was at the pinnacle he'd savored throughout his adult lifetime. Almost there. And then, crash! It was gone. All of it. He was totally defeated.

This was our tenth counseling session. I had discussed most of the truths in this book with him repeatedly. He could articulate quite well the principles he was learning, but to my knowledge he never appropriated them. They remained just "information" to him, "interesting insights."

The only thing this dear brother wanted to discuss in our sessions was how he could recoup his losses. As far as I could discern, he never gave up his fleshly yearning for the honors of men. He longed for human acceptance and fleshly-generated self-esteem.

Satan's Favorite Road
As with this deceived brother, a great deal of your flesh was generated by your efforts to get your need for acceptance and

self-acceptance satisfied by extracting it out of people and the world system. You see, Christ was not number one with this pastor; his job and prestige were. It is my conviction that Satan's *most effective tool* against Christians is to deceive them into continuing to use their old, green highways to satisfy this need we all have for love and self-esteem.

Jesus desires that we look to Him as *the* source, moment by moment, to supply this as well as all our needs. Once we're called out to Him, He lovingly begins to woo us away as His bride from our "former lovers" through which we sought to get our needs supplied.

Spiritual Descendants of Gomer

We hear a lot about the necessity for "brokenness," but it seems that some of us have a hazy understanding of what we must be broken *from*. God seeks to destroy our Lord-of-the-Ring ways. They are harlotry! Often He has to allow suffering that our flesh can't handle to come into our lives in order to break us. The book of Hosea presents a graphic typological study of this process.

Chapter 1 tells of the Lord's command to Hosea to marry a whore. I don't understand why learned men argue over whether or not this is literal. The Bible says very clearly in verse 2 that it was the Lord's command to Hosea, and it fits perfectly into the book's purpose as a typological study. Hosea obediently married Gomer, who proved to be woefully unfaithful to his commitment to her. That's a picture of God and the nation Israel; Christ and His bride, the Church; and Christ and you as an individual.

Gomer bore children by her various lovers as she flitted from one to another, seeking to get her needs supplied in ways other than her husband. Sexual intercourse was not Gomer's primary goal, but simply a means to an end. She was trading herself to her lovers, allowing them to use her so she could get all her needs supplied. Likewise we, too, are tempted to return to our fleshly techniques in order to satisfy our need for love.

Let's pick up the story in Chapter 2, verse 5: "For their mother has played the harlot. For she said, 'I will go after my lovers, who give me my bread and my water, my wool and my flax, my oil and my drink.'" Gomer was continuing to use her old techniques to milk her needs supply from the world system. This is a picture of the contemporary Christian who strives to climb the corporate ladder, denominational ladder, athletic ladder, club ladder, or whatever to generate and maintain acceptance and self-acceptance.

"Walking after the flesh" could range from clinging to physical beauty to striving for perfectionism in performance; from displaying Christmas cards from the "right people" to craving to be invited to the party where many of the "in" group at the church will be gathering tonight; from striving to acquire the house with the right address so you can "feel good" about where you live to having to have your hair look "just right" before you can feel "comfortable" going out; from name dropping to *having* to have a snappy car or clothes or boat to feel better about yourself. Ad infinitum! All these things are fleshly techniques for obtaining acceptance and self-esteem from the system rather than from the Lord, your husband. It's infidelity! There is nothing evil about many of these things *per se*. It's the *motive* that is not of God.

Jesus, the committed Husband, reveals His divine plan for wooing His bride away from all competition. He fixes things so that flesh trips cease to be productive. He dries up the supply so His bride will wake up and turn to the one who really loves her instead of chasing after those who are looking to her as *their* needs supply.

The End of the Road

God was going to make Gomer's flesh less productive than before.

> I will hedge up her way with thorns, and I will build a wall against her so that she cannot find her paths [old ways] (Hos. 2:6).

Christian, are you experiencing a diminishing return on *your* efforts lately in terms of the satisfactions you formerly derived? Are you traveling on "old roads"?

"And she will pursue her lovers"—she was reluctant to give up this "good" thing she had going for her—"but she will not

overtake them; and she will seek them, but will not find them."
Then she will say

> I will go back to my first husband, for it was better for me then
> than now! (Hos. 2:7).

Jesus likewise allows you to walk in your old ways, patiently
wooing you and suffering through your infidelities to Him. He
tearfully watches as you look to your former ways of extracting
your needs supply out of the world system, ways you learned so
well prior to the marriage (salvation). Then He allows you to
begin experiencing a diminishing return on your efforts.

At first the unfaithful wife's prayers are centered on asking
the Lord to defeat the devil and restore her "victorious life."
Sound like any TV programs you've heard? As her fleshly effort
weakens in productivity, she usually becomes frantic, believing
the devil's lie that the Lord must have put her on hold to take
care of more-pressing matters. She often begs Him to hear her
plea, which seems to be falling on deaf ears. Oh, but He's lovingly working.

Jesus, Our Source

Finally, the adulterous bride realizes there is something drastically wrong in her life. It's at this point that she is most recep-
tive to "returning to her first love," Christ, her Bridegroom, to
adore Him (see Rev. 2:4) and seek Him alone as her source.

> For she does not know that it was I who gave her the grain, the
> new wine, and the oil, and lavished on her silver and gold
> [which she misused] (Hos. 2:8).

She just thought she was getting her needs supplied by her
fleshly effort, but it was God who was supplying all the time. She
thought her life would surely be a disaster without her source,
the thing she had always depended on.

> "Therefore, I will take back *My* grain . . . and *My* new wine.
> *My* wool and *My* flax," the Lord said (Hos. 2:9, emphasis
> added).

It all belongs to our Husband. "The earth is the *Lord's* and all
it contains" (Psalm 24:1).

Hosea 2:10,11 says that God vowed to put an end to Gomer's ability to even *marginally* satisfy her needs through the flesh. It might even get so "bad" (from her perspective) that she would despair of life itself. This was what was happening to the lady who wrote the suicide note which began this book.

Can you discern with spiritual eyes how a well-meaning but unbroken, world-system-trained Christian counselor actually defeats God's purpose if he "helps" such a "self-sufficient" person by making his fleshly techniques more productive? The client might get "better," but he is working against the Holy Spirit's goal of weakening the flesh. Hosea 2:12 states that Gomer's supply that she credited to the flesh's efforts would be destroyed.

Then God said,

> I will allure her, *bring* her into the wilderness, and speak kindly to her (Hos. 2:14).

Why? Did you ever consider how well your flesh will supply your needs in the wilderness? Let's say that you have a fancy address, you come from the "right" family, or your bumper sticker boasts you are a native-born citizen of the "right" state. How much good will these things do you in the wilderness? The only people you can try to impress out there are the jack rabbits! You're going to find one source and only one out there, and that's Jesus. He is your only hope in the wilderness. Everything else is unproductive. He will take you there because He *loves* you, not because He's mad at you.

God finally hemmed Gomer into the box canyon of unproductive flesh, "I will give her her vineyards [supply] from there," He said (Hos. 2:15). He had to take her to a point of despair before He could trust her to know who her source was. This way she got the message loud and clear that her flesh could not meet her needs.

Then God further stated, "The valley of Achor [will be her] door of hope" (Hos. 2:15). The valley of Achor is where Achan, the man who stole the forbidden "needs supply" at Ai, was executed in Joshua 7. Israel's (and Gomer's) fleshly effort had to be dealt with before she could move forward into an intimate walk with the Lord as His beloved wife. Dear people of God, verse 15 says,

> *Then* I will give her her vineyards from *there*, and the valley of Achor as a *door of hope* (emphasis added).

Achor means "trouble." God has to bring a Christian to the end of the "trusted old ways" before she will turn from her "former lovers" to Him alone. This is often painful but always essential.

The Desert Song

Though God frequently has to accomplish this discipline through trauma, look at the results:

> She will sing there as in the days of her youth [salvation], as in the day when she came up from the land of Egypt (Hos. 2:15*b*).

Whatever "song" is on the lips of the Christian who has yet to come to the end of the flesh's resources is like the latest tune to hit the top forty. It comes with about a thirty-day warranty. *The only permanent, lasting song that any Christian will experience on this planet — the only one with a lifetime guarantee — is the one she learns to sing in the valley of Achor, where she comes to the end of depending on her flesh.* This may happen in different ways for different Christians. There will be different degrees of suffering for different folks. It's all relative, and God is the one in control. He never *causes* it, but He allows it, and its purpose is love. He's taking you to a deeper level of oneness. This is not something to fear. It is simply a matter of keeping your eyes of faith on Jesus. He is totally committed to your best welfare.

My Husband

"And it will come about in *that* day, declares the Lord, that *you* will call Me 'my Husband' and will no longer call Me 'my Master'" (Hos. 2:16, NASB margin). She has been His beloved wife all along, but *she hasn't recognized who she is.* God has called her by her true name (beloved wife) ever since the relationship began, but she saw Him as a burdensome master. She had to experience the valley of Achor before she began to call Him "my Husband." She never appropriated her identity until she got caught in the box canyon of Achor where her flesh stopped yielding its usual productive return.

Look at verses 19 and 20:

> And *I* will betroth you to Me *forever*; yes, *I* will betroth you to *Me* in righteousness and in justice, in lovingkindness and in

compassion, and *I* will betroth you to Me in faithfulness. *Then* you will *know* the *Lord* (emphasis added).

Christian, is your life humdrum? Does your husband not appreciate all the things you do for him? Do your kids take you for granted? Does your wife seem to expect more than you feel you can possibly deliver? Does it seem that no matter how hard you try, your boss has always got another "if only" chinning bar for you to pull on? Is your earthsuit wearing out, and the jogging you thought would surely help hasn't overcome the force of gravity? Did the deal for your dream house fall through? Are you widowed? Are you facing retirement, horrified at the prospect of having no "purpose" left in life? Do you fear death? Does no one seem to understand you? Have your friends or even family turned away from you? Do your years seem to have been wasted as you conduct "instant replays" of your life?

Dear, unhappy bride of Christ. If you are *under* the load, you are in the Valley of Achor. Stop trying to milk your needs supply out of this world by the flesh. *That's the wrong spouse.* You *are* loved. You're the beloved bride who has "no spot or wrinkle or any such thing; but . . . [is] holy and blameless" (Eph. 5:27).

Turn from leaning on the "trustworthiness" of *your* talent, *your* attractive earthsuit, *your* spiritual gifts, *your* intelligence, *your* position, *your* popularity, *your* good job, *your* financial security, *your* good marriage, and *your* obedient kids as your *primary* means of generating and maintaining your inner peace and satisfaction in this life. That's playing the whore! It's fine that you have been blessed by your Husband with all the above, but don't concentrate on that. *Remember who you are, and concentrate on and praise your Husband.*

You are the totally loved, chosen, called-out, holy, virgin (see 2 Cor. 11:2), blameless, righteous bride of the Lord Jesus Christ. Imagine your infinite worth! Your Bridegroom has promised by His blood to supply all your needs (see Phil. 4:19). You will never be a worn-out, old wife, cast aside for some younger lover. You are loved, totally loved with a loyalty unprecedented, by the God of the universe. He has and continues to identify you this way ever since you gave yourself to Him at salvation when you repented of your old life of rebellious independence and agreed to the marriage terms.

You entered into a oneness relationship with your spiritual Husband, but you must agree with His view (the only true view) and walk with Him as His beloved if you would experience abundant life on this planet. The music and lyrics of this song are usually born in the valley of Achor. It often takes that to get us to turn loose of the old ways.

Questions for Further Study

1. What is one reason God will take a Christian to the wilderness of life?

2. Do you think it is possible for a Christian to really know Christ as life and source if there aren't some wilderness troubles along the way? Explain your thinking on this question.

3. As you have finished reading this chapter, what practical steps can you take if you find yourself in the Valley of Achor?

TWELVE

GOD'S ULTIMATE
PURPOSE FOR YOU

"Oh, Bill, I'm so free! Free in Christ! Free at last! Oh, why couldn't I see all this before. It's so plain to me in Scripture, now that I know what to look for! It's all so marvelous!"

The dear lady was beside herself with reveling in her new found righteousness in Christ. She'd spent her whole Christian life striving to become something she had always been since salvation. For years she had fought a war that Jesus had already won for her. She'd discovered that her victory is to be appropriated by faith in His work, not earned by hers.

"But Bill," she said, "if I'm already holy, blameless, accepted, righteous, and all those other wonderful adjectives I see in God's Word, what's the purpose in God's leaving me here? Why doesn't He just take me home?"

That's a good question and the answer is glorious! Oh, the fantastic opportunity that lies before you between now and the time you go home! You and I have been offered the privilege of preparing ourselves for our future roles in the celestial order God has planned. Earth is very much like graduate school or an NFL training camp. We're all winners in Christ already, but we have only one opportunity to train for our eternal leadership role, and it's here on planet earth.

Why He Hasn't "Beamed Us Up"

To explain why God doesn't just "beam us up" as they do in *Star Trek*, we'll have to digress a bit to get the big picture of God's plan for you. We'll begin with your physical birth and represent this event by placing the word *birth* above the base of the triangle in Figure 12.1.

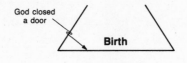

Figure 12.1

When you were born, God closed a door behind you so you could never cross back over that threshold. Let's face it, a person can never cease to exist. We'll let the base of the triangle in Figure 12.1 represent the closed door. God has established this limit that we cannot cross. Job 14:5 says, "[Man's] days are determined, the number of his months is with Thee, and his limits Thou hast set so that he cannot pass." Our God is the keeper of the door, and when He closes a door, it's *closed*.

God's plan for you was to draw you to Himself (see 2 Pet. 3:9). To accomplish this, He established limits around you to "crowd" you toward making a decision to submit to Christ. This is not an abrasive teaching, but a beautiful love story of our Lord's wooing His bride to Himself. We'll let the apex of the triangle in Figure 12.2 represent salvation, and the two sides the circumstances, or limits, that crowd you toward the decision to receive Jesus as Lord and Savior.

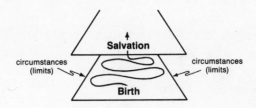

Figure 12.2

Perhaps you can recall an episode from your past where in the midst of your sin you worked yourself into such a pickle that you did a 180 degree turn, vowing to reform, motivated by the painful experience. That was one of those limits beyond which God wouldn't let *you* go. Others went beyond, but you turned back toward a more middle-of-the road position. You over-corrected and traveled too far, however, until God let you bump your nose on yet another of His limits. Your pathway as you bumped back and forth between His limits *for you* led you to a confrontation with Jesus Christ unto salvation.

Let's presume that you chose to repent and accept Jesus Christ as Savior and Lord. Once you did, God slammed another door behind you. I believe that just as a person cannot cease to have been born physically, so he cannot cease to have been born spiritually. Keeping him in this position is God's business, and He is well able to do so (see Phil. 1:6).

I will quickly confess that some folks who are truly born from above perform as though they are still in the bottom triangle. But when they do, our Father will discipline them by tightening up the circumstances around them until they begin to act more like they've been born anew (Heb. 12:9).

God's goal in all this is clearly revealed in Romans 8:29: "For whom He foreknew, He also predestined to become conformed to the image of His Son, that He might be the first-born among many brethren." His plan is to conform us to the image of Christ. Can anything bring more excitement to your heart? He isn't going to accomplish this *after* we die, with physical death being the agent of change, but here on earth with the Holy Spirit being the agent of change.

Notice that word "predestined." That means God is going to do it to you. You've been placed into the loving obstacle course, and the Lord is hard at work conforming you. What's more, He says that He is going to finish what He started with you (Phil. 1:6).

God has two plans for accomplishing His goal. Plan A is for you to see truth in the Word and respond in faith and obedience. I find, however, that most of us Christians are mentally retarded. We see a verse such as "Pray without ceasing" (1 Thess. 5:17) and respond with "How can I do that? I can't pray continually and still accomplish my work." So God has to revert to Plan B, Romans 8:28. He has to let a little "all things" come into a person's life. He tightens the limits up around a person to box him into a more dependent position.

God hates independence. He wants you to be *de*pendent on Him as Jesus was. So He'll let something happen to jerk the rug out from under a person's self-sufficiency, then show him the alternative of opting for Christ's sufficiency. Through this trauma, the person will learn how to pray without ceasing and accomplish his work simultaneously. In fact, he'll learn that this is the easier way to fly. He will have "entered into God's rest" by trusting Christ to accomplish the work through him.

Jesus Christ was the most dependent person who ever lived. Many fail to see it. They see Him in His earthwalk as self-sufficient, when actually He was totally dependent on another. "The Father abiding in Me does His works," Jesus said (John 14:10). Thus, since our Father has dedicated Himself to the task of conforming us to the image of Christ, the circumstances of this planet are *designed* to bring the Christian person to the end of *his* sufficiency.

Stop fighting it, brother. Give up all your "rights" — all talents, all abilities, all gifts, all the things you've clung to to get your need met for self-acceptance. You'll love the results! You will find "life" through allowing Him to express Himself through your talents, your abilities, your gifts, and your personality to a

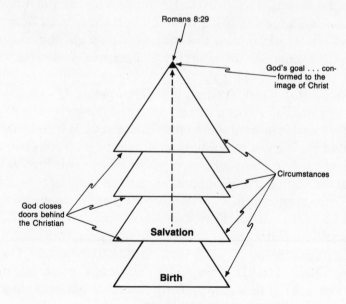

Figure 12.3

hurting world to do *His* will. That's the way Jesus walked. He let the Father do it through Him.

Step By Step

Needless to say, maturity doesn't occur in one giant leap, but through a process. "But we all . . . are being transformed into the same image from glory to glory" (2 Cor. 3:18). Figure 12.3 depicts the evolution into the image of Christ for the believer. The escalating triangles represent the various growth stages Christians experience as they participate in the conforming process.

Once a person is born from above, his nature is already Christlike, but it's infantile in maturity. He is like an oak sapling that can mature into a fully grown oak tree. He is not half oak and half briar bush. And by faith and obedience, as he begins to act consistently with his new nature, he will look more and more like Jesus.

Of course, a Christian can just as surely "walk after the flesh" and develop character that is completely contrary to his true nature. This will then be burned at the Judgment Seat of Christ, but the man himself will be saved, as we saw earlier. As this person ages, his character will evolve contrary to his godly nature. Such a person will be limited in his training for leadership in the future, heavenly realm, because his earthwalk was spent trusting in the arm of his flesh. He'll be fitted into the "house not made with hands, eternal in the heavens" (2 Cor. 5:1) as a sapling instead of as a mature tree.

The same will be true for the person with "good, socially accepted" flesh who misses the course on strength through weakness. Earth is the place for learning to walk in dependence, not heaven. Such a person will automatically revert to dependency in heaven, but there will be no reward for it.

Those who develop Christian character here will occupy positions of leadership in all that our creative Father has planned in the future, eternal social order. Those who have been "faithful with a few things . . . will [be] put . . . in charge of many things" (Matt. 25:23). (For some exciting insight into our role in heaven, see Paul Billheimer's *Don't Waste Your Sorrows*, published by Christian Literature Crusade.)

Doors, Doors, Doors

I have no idea how many spiritual plateaus there are through which the Holy Spirit can lead the believer. But when the pilgrim chooses with his will to commit to the new step, God closes the door behind him. Slam. You cannot back out. You can act like you're backing out, but if you really had your teeth gritted when you threw your will switch, He slammed that door behind you. It's as serious as a marriage vow to Him. Later on, if you buy into sin's temptations to back out, you leave God no alternative but to switch to Plan B. He'll have to let a little "all things" come into your life.

Total Commitment

One door we must pass through if we are to go on with God is total commitment (Figure 12.4). I used to think that total commitment was performance-based. For example, I thought preachers were more totally committed than truck drivers. Some years later, however, I began to counsel a pastor or two who weren't totally committed and some truck drivers who were.

Figure 12.4

Total commitment is coming to the point where you are willing to place nothing between you and the Lord. "Lord Jesus, I give You my wife," I prayed. "You may do anything that seems good to You with Anabel. She is Your property, not mine, and owners have the right to do whatever they wish with their property." I must do this with everything.

"So here they are, Lord, my wife, my kids, their health, myself, my health, my house, my bucks, my career, my physical appearance, my will, everything! I will place nothing between me and You. I commit it all to You." And He slams the door behind you. You are now totally committed. It's a one-time decision that you make with your will, with your teeth gritted. It then becomes His job to choreograph the circumstances of your life to make your decision experientially real to you (see Phil. 1:6; 2:13).

Remember the pastor I wrote about who lost the big church, his reputation, and his future high denominational office because he was caught in adultery? He wasn't totally committed. You see, he still had Jesus, but Christ was not number one. Those other things were more important to him.

The Last Major Door

I believe the Lord has shown me what the last major door is. It's claiming the Cross (see Figure 12.5). When the Lord said, "Take up [your] Cross daily, and follow Me" (Luke 9:23), He didn't mean you must become a preacher. The Cross is not an instrument of service; it's an instrument of death. When you step across *this* threshold on your pilgrimage, you have got to hold a funeral. Your own!

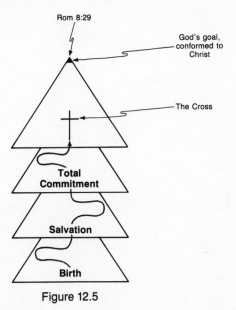

Figure 12.5

Let me reiterate, you do not attempt to crucify yourself. Nor do you attempt to "die to self." That is a misnomer. There is no such teaching in the Word. You do not die to anything; you simply agree with God's Word that you already *have*. But this is not just giving intellectual assent to some concept. This is as serious as getting married. You cannot enter into it lightly. You've got to grit your teeth and say, "I mean it, Lord." For many, a house has to fall on them before they'll give in. For others, it's a quiet commitment. When you do, He will slam the door behind you. You will have entered into *claiming* your true identity in Christ.

Accompanying every new commitment by the believer is a time of testing. This time is not so God can determine how I am going to respond to my new commitment. He already knows. Rather, the testing time is for *me* to know if I am going to stay hitched. The only way I can really know that is when it gets hot in the kitchen.

Testing is purposeful. So when it happens, just praise Him and get with the program. If you kick at it, you flunk the course and have to start over. It's easy to praise the Lord when everything's cool, but you can "offer up a sacrifice of praise" (Heb. 13:15) only when it's not. A sacrifice costs something. It hurts to give it. Praising the Lord when you feel bad is not being a phony either; it's being obedient. Your heart can be in it even when your emotions are not.

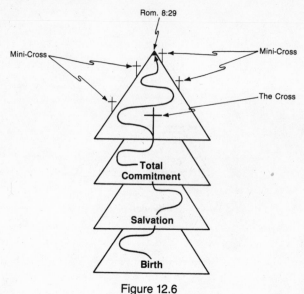

Figure 12.6

I have depicted these testing times from the Cross toward your becoming conformed to the image of Christ as mini-Crosses (see Figure 12.6). These are daily choices when you will be faced with choosing either Channel #1 or Channel #2. You can either buy into the deception and blow it, or you can say, "I know where that's coming from! I'm dead to you! Buzz off!" Then you appropriate truth.

A Cross of Closet Doors

Anabel and I used to live in a house that had sliding closet doors. She liked those doors kept shut; I liked mine open. Anabel frequently made a poignant plea for me to shut my doors when I finished dressing. Sometimes I would, sometimes I wouldn't. I hadn't the faintest notion that there was any spiritual dimension to our door preferences.

I will never forget one particular Saturday morning in that house. I was getting a jacket out of my closet when something "said" to me, "the door." I thought "Aw!" and walked out of the room and down the hall. Something again "said" to me, "the door." Oh, oh. I figured that must be the Holy Spirit. Let's face it, it wasn't the power of sin.

So I stopped. Notice: *I* stopped. Nothing stopped me. I'm not a robot. I chose to stop and believe that the Lord was speaking to me, that He wanted to use me to close the doors for Anabel. It had never occurred to Delbert Dumb here that all those years Anabel had been saying, "Honey, please love me the way Christ loves His wife by closing the closet doors for me so the room will look pretty." It actually says I'm supposed to do that right there in Ephesians 5:25: "Husbands, close the closet doors for your wives, just as Jesus also loved His wife." But I never knew that! I didn't know that was a way to love Anabel. I'm convinced I am mentally retarded when it comes to knowing how to love Anabel. But praise His wonderful name, He is teaching me how to love her, how to make restitution for all those years of hell that I dished out to her.

As I stopped in the hallway, however, sin said to me, "That's *my* closet. If I want to leave the doors open, that's my business. No woman is going to control me." But there was that gentle knowing that Jesus desires to love Anabel through me. I was at a mini-Cross. I was being given the opportunity to *act* "dead to sin and alive to God," love Anabel, and pile up points for the Judgment Seat of Christ. Conversely, I could *act* dead to God and alive to sin, piling up more wood, hay, and stubble for the big wiener roast in the sky.

So I said, "Okay, Jesus, I'm going to let You close the doors for Anabel." And I set one foot in front of the other back into the bedroom and slid the doors shut, *believing* it was Him doing it through me.

Now, I confess that I had closed closet doors on many occasions prior to this incident, but then my attitude was more like "Dumb doors! Stupid wife! Okay, I'll close the stupid doors if that's what it takes to keep the peace!" I was living under law, the law of I should, I have to, I must, I ought to, it's my duty.

There have also been those occasions when I have closed the closet doors this way: "Maybe if I do something nice for her today, she'll do something nice for me tonight." That's the flesh for certain. It's nothing but plying her with closet-door-closing. Lost guys do the same thing with their wives.

This time, however, I claimed the truth of who I am — that I am delighted to offer myself to Christ to allow Him to express love to Anabel through me. There was no animosity, no frustration, no hidden agenda for bedtime. I was resting and at peace within.

Some guy says, "I sure wish he'd get past these Mickey Mouse illustrations and get on to explaining how to experience the victorious Christian life." Hey, that *is* the victorious Christian life. You would not believe how many hundreds of hours of my marriage I have wasted over such things as closet doors, but now I'm free. Free to obey the law of love. Free to close doors. You can't believe how good it feels! And remember Jesus' statement that, those who are faithful in little things will be entrusted with much (see Appendix H).

Brokenness, the Key to Leadership
The number of broken people in the Bible who learned to walk in dependency upon God is so obvious. *Only a broken person is fit for leadership in the Kingdom of God.* You can bank on it. Show me an unbroken Christian, and I'll show you a person who is

leaning on the arm of the flesh to accomplish the task. Show me an unbroken Christian and *I'll show you a person who is milking his need for acceptance and self-acceptance out of his work.* He *needs* the work. Take it away from him and he'll get depressed. You see, Jesus wasn't the source from whom he was drawing his esteem; it was the work.

Paul's work was removed from him the last few years of his life. His goal for evangelizing Spain was gone. He was a hard charger, but he didn't get depressed over the lost goal. He wrote his most encouraging letters from this place of "nonachievement." He was able to do it because he wasn't milking his need out of the achieving of tangible goals. His major goal was "that I may know Him, and the power of His resurrection" (Phil. 3:10). He drew even *closer* to his goal while experiencing the *in*activity of prison life. Again, I challenge you, Christian. What is the source of your acceptance of yourself? How are you getting *your* needs met? What or who is the source of your purpose in life? *How much can the Lord remove from you and you'll continue to praise Him and rest* in the acceptance that's yours in Christ?

You Are a Topic of Conversation

The devil accuses Christians before the Father day and night (see Rev. 12:10). If you are born from above, you are the topic of many of those discussions.

Allow me to take the liberty, through Job's, Peter's, and other experiences, to speculate on how such a conversation could go. The Lord might say, "Have you considered My servant, (your name)? I'm so proud of that child. If I only had more like (your name), you would see a different Church on planet earth!"

Whereupon the accuser might respond, "Oh, yes? Let me tell you what *I* know about (your name)! The only reason he continues to praise You is that it pays off. So long as he 'pays his dues,' You keep his life running smoothly. You let me touch that darling spot, that thing he feels he couldn't live without, that thing that *You have given him,* that came from Your hand. Let me attack it, and I'll prove to You what (your name) is made of! He'll reject You!"

This is the timing the Father has planned. It is time to move you a step "*from* glory *to* glory." The one with the nail-scarred hand inserts the key into the lock to the protective hedge and says, "You may do thus and so, but you may not do this and that." He gives the Evil One permission to *attack the flesh*. God allows him to undermine the "righteousness" (acceptance) in which you formerly trusted so that you can learn to opt for the righteousness from above based on faith in Jesus Christ.

Please do not recoil from this teaching. Don't sell out to to-day's popular "prosperity gospel." That is such error. It falls so far short of the true riches that God has for all who are in Christ. Don't kick against your loving Father's refining process. He is allowing your circumstances to chip away all dependence on the arm of the flesh. You are so beautiful as the new person you truly are in Christ! See it! Get the vision of it from God's Word to you. Believe it and appropriate it as your own. As my friend Jack Taylor says, "Don't be afraid. When you see who you actually *are* down deep in your heart as a new creation in Christ—you will like what you see!" And as you allow Christ to express His life through you, you will attain a self-esteem that will be unsinkable.

God speed, dear friend. I don't know you. I have never seen you, but I'm proud with a godly joy that you are my relative in Christ. I'm praying for you as you read this book. I pray you will experience great victory in this life to the glory of our lovely Jesus. I want our eyes to meet at the Judgment Seat of Christ as we both hear our Lord say, "Well done." There will be tears of joy in my eyes for you as I see Christ honor you as they do the young people who stand erect on the champions' podium at the Olympics. I'll be so proud of you if you have appropriated Him as your life to glorify Him. "If one member is honored, all the members rejoice with it" (1 Cor. 12:26). I'm pulling for you! Keep pressing on! By *His* grace You can do it. God is faithful. "And stand [you] *will*, for the Lord is able to *make* [you] stand" (Rom. 14:4*b*, emphasis added).

> To Him who is able to do *exceeding abundantly beyond all* that we ask or think, according to the power that works *within* us, to *Him* be the glory (Eph. 3:20, 21, emphasis added).

Turn forward now to the next page and look at the "Death/Life Certificate." My prayer is that you will sign it as an indication of the intent of your heart. God bless you.

Death/Life Certificate

My dear Jesus,

I confess that I have occupied a throne that is rightfully Yours. I drew a circle around myself and declared myself "Lord of the Ring." I have tried to control the variables in my life, pursuing the goal of getting my needs met.

I now see that when You died, I died, my old sin nature who refused to let You be Lord of my Ring. When you were raised, You enabled a brand-new me to be born, a new me who loves You and is holy, righteous, and blameless *in* You. I now submit myself totally to You to express Your life through me to do Your will on earth. I have no rights. I own nothing. Even I have been bought with Your blood and body, and I have been set aside for Your purpose and delight.

I mean this, Jesus. I claim by faith that the old me is extinct and that as the new me, the real me, I have everything I need in You to face life. I know You will permit this commitment to be tested, but I trust You in that as well. I have no hidden agenda or deals up my sleeve. I *know* You have my best interests at heart. You are a fantastic Savior, and I trust You.

I love you,

_____   _____
                Name   Date

Questions for Further Study

1. Explain how God's love can allow tough circumstances to come into the walk of one of His children.

2. Spend a few minutes reflecting on your struggles and hardships. How are they being used by God to conform you to the image of Christ?

3. Has there been a point of total commitment in your life where God shut the door behind you?

4. Has there been a point where you appropriated the Cross, your death, burial, and resurrection in Christ, and God slammed a door behind you? If so, let me encourage you to recount these experiences in your mind, then write down a brief summary as a personal reminder. If you haven't made these imperative decisions, please do so right now.

Summary

It would be an excellent and beneficial summary to return to the questions at the end of each chapter, reviewing the questions and your answers. They will only become yours through study, prayer, and repetition as you trust the Lord to teach you.

"To taste of the grace of God is one thing; to be established in it and manifest it in character, habit, and regular life, is another."
— Miles Stanford

APPENDIXES

APPENDIX A

Jesus said, "Greater works than these shall he do" (John 14:12). Christ is the Vine, we are the branches. There is no qualitative difference in the life of the vine and the life of the branch. It is not "vine life" and "branch life," but *the* Life. It's not the duty of the branch to try his hardest to produce fruit. Branches simply abide in the vine, and the fruit-bearing takes place as a normal process. Which can produce the greater works? A vine alone with one branch or that same vine with millions of branches abiding in the vine? You see, it's not greater quality Christ made reference to, but greater quantity.

APPENDIX B

God exempts small children from being responsible for their condition as Adam's heirs. He considers them innocent. Jesus makes their condition very clear in Matthew 18:10: "I say to you, that their [small children's] angels in heaven continually behold the face of My Father who is in heaven." Do you know of any Biblical teaching that indicates lost people have a personal angel? No, children belong to God until such time as they become responsible for their condition.

Jesus goes on to say that they'll "fall into sin," and He warns those who lead them into sin that they are accountable for misleading them. Then He tells the parable of the lost sheep. This is a portrayal of the Holy Spirit's searching for someone who is lost. Tell me, what is the definition of "lost"? It means "I *used* to own it, but I lost it."

Do you see it? All little children belong to God initially, then subsequently through the maturation process *get* lost, then they have the opportunity to *get* saved as a choice of their will by accepting Jesus' atonement.

APPENDIX C

Many of you reading this book have already accepted Jesus Christ as Savior and Lord. If you haven't, it is our sincere prayer that you will very soon. For those of you who have, as you journeyed along on your Main Street, one day you came to the building marked "S" (for salvation) and accepted Christ as your Savior. As previously stated, this didn't surprise God, since He saw your whole street before the world began. True, *you* made the choice with your will to accept Christ, but it didn't surprise God when you did it. He's omniscient and not limited to the time dimension like you. He knows the future.

This in no way means that certain lost men have no option to get saved. That's confusing the issue by attempting to mix the helicopter view with the Main Street view. You can't do that in my opinion. How can you consider time and nontime simultaneously? It seems to me we must reflect on but one of these views at a time in our human state or we'll end up with fatalism, believing that we have no choice; that if you're number is not on God's list it's tough luck for you. I don't see that in the Word. God doesn't manipulate us against our will. To do so would make us robots and give Him no pleasure.

APPENDIX D

First Corinthians 12:9 states that some are given the spiritual gift of faith. These folks have been singled out by the Lord and given this spiritual gift for building up the body of Christ, not for "believing God for a Jaguar." The rest of us Christians have simply been given what the Bible calls "a measure of faith" (Rom. 12:3). It is my conviction that some Christian teachers do not comprehend that they've been given the *gift* of faith. Thus, mistakenly assuming they have ordinary faith like every other Christian, they build a ministry around exhorting believers to get more faith to acquire Rolex watches and guaranteed health.

They mean well. I don't intend to fault their motives, just their message. Many times, I have had the experience of counseling those whose lives were shipwrecked from striving to generate more faith as a result of listening to this teaching. You don't need to beg for more faith. You have all the faith you need to walk in the fullness of the Spirit.

APPENDIX E

Do you recall when King David sinned by numbering Israel in 1 Chronicles 21? Verse one says, "Satan stood up against Israel and moved David to number Israel." How did Satan do that? Did he say, "Well, David, it looks like a good, clear day for counting heads. Why not go ahead and do it?" Oh, no, it couldn't have been done so overtly to this man who had a heart to do God's will. He had to deceive him into doing it.

It's my conviction that Satan gave David the idea through his brain with first-person-singular pronouns and an Israeli accent. David swallowed the idea because he had man-o-war flesh, and that sort of flesh always *feels* more comfortable when he knows what his "strength" is. God was his strength, but he was deceived into placing his faith in the wrong object—numbers. That's why God told him not to take a census.

APPENDIX F

A Christian whom I greatly respect commented concerning the use of the illustration, "This example of cooking eggs seems so trivial. How about an example of struggling with some habitual sin? Your example may produce a lot of guilt such as 'You mean every little detail of my life is a spiritual test? Good grief! Don't I ever get to relax?'"

Dear people, independent living is what sin is all about. An independent lifestyle is trusting in the arm of the flesh. Jesus never struck off on His own as if He needed a breather from intimacy with the Father. We, too, were created for intimate union and are being conformed to His image, lovingly drawn into the net of living "in vital union with Him" (Col. 2:6b, TLB).

The Christian who feels he needs daily spiritual coffee breaks is experiencing religion, not relationship. Religion is a chore; relationship is a well-spring of living water within.

APPENDIX G

There is *one* thing all believers can do equally well as we begin each day. That is to offer all that we are to Christ to express His Life through us, to use us to do *His* will. Our ability to do this is not related to how many spiritual gifts we have or our talent, I.Q., appearance, wealth, charisma, wisdom, or circumstances. True, we're stewards of all these, but we begin each day having an equal opportunity with all believers, including those with the highest and the lowest exposure in the Church.

The believer who suffers great trial due to political persecution, marital stress, and so on finds that God simply makes greater grace available to him to allow Christ to handle it through him.

Believing you have no worthwhile opportunity because you have a low profile when compared to world-renowned Christians is a lie. You can perhaps gain more rewards than the world's highest-profile Christian leader. The ground is level at the beginning of each day.

The housewife who yields herself to Christ to develop a happy home, husband, and children will receive the "Well done" not because the results are perfect, but because the method was. The work will be identical to the Foundation: Christ's life as she collaborated with Him.

APPENDIX H

God *is* God, and He runs the universe, which in one sense is simply a big laboratory. He is carefully controlling all the variables here, and they're designed to bring people to salvation and conform them to Christ's image. Even the devil has a role in this process. It was no shock to God when Lucifer rebelled. He didn't say, "Oh, My soul! How did *that* happen." When God finishes using Satan as a part of the whole refining process for Christians, He'll end his activity in a split second.

Look at Job 1. The Lord and Satan were having one of their daily conversations when *God* brought up the subject of Job. If He'd never mentioned Job's situation, the book of Job would never have occurred. God did not cause Job's misery, as He is not the instigator of evil. But He surely gave His permission for it to happen, and its purpose was to conform Job to the image of Christ.

The Father began by saying, "Have you considered My servant Job?" (paraphrasing). "What a fine man he is! I wish I had a whole world full of people like him! He loves Me and submits to My authority over him."

Whereupon Satan responded (just as God knew he would), "Well, the only reason Job responds to Your authority over him is that it pays off for him. You've got a hedge [protective angels] built around him so nothing bad can happen to him. You let it stop paying dividends and watch how fast he stops praising and submitting. *Job has You on a performance-based acceptance*; so long as You keep performing the way *he* wants, he'll 'pay You off' with praise. *He* is in control of *You*, not vice versa. You give me permission to wipe out what You've done for him and watch how fast he stops praising You."

God said, "Okay, you can do thus and so to him, but you can't do this and that." Note that God still maintained control.

He simply moved the limits Satan could not transgress. He didn't let Satan touch Job.

God was about to do something beautiful in Job. He was bringing Job to the end of himself—of *his* rights, of *self-justification*, of milking his acceptance out of the community, and of self-esteem based on his ability. It would be a painful experience for Job, but when you get to talk to him about it one day, he will assure you that he wouldn't take anything for having gone through it.

Once given the opportunity, Satan utterly wiped out Job's family and possessions. (Note that he could have killed his wife, too, as she was not included in God's "exclusions," but he didn't because he desired to use her later on. He knew he could control her when the time was ripe.)

Chapter 1 ends by stating that Job praised the Lord through it all. He came through like gangbusters. Even though praising the Lord was not "paying dividends" as before, he continued to submit.

You'd think the Lord would have rested His case, but in the second chapter He did it again. "Well, what do you think of Job now," He might have said. "There's no one like him on the earth, a blameless and upright man who reveres Me and turns away from evil. And he still holds fast his integrity, although *you* incited Me against him, to ruin him without cause."

The devil replied, "Yes, but You didn't let me touch his *body*. Put Your hand out and touch his bone and his flesh, and I'll bet he's soon cursing You." Note that in all this time, Satan never said "*I'll* do thus and so," because he is helpless to act outside of God's authority. He knows that, *which is saying a lot more for him than one can say about some Christians*. Again God gave him permission to carry out the dirty work, but He established more limits beyond which Satan could not transgress (he was told he couldn't kill Job). God's goal is to attack the flesh, the old ways to which the Christian clings. The believer must be brought to the point of releasing those things, no matter how darling they may be to him. So, for forty more chapters, Satan beat on Job.

Beware of falling into the trap of heeding the Evil One's accusations against God when it looks as though He is allowing circumstances that aren't for your best interests. Never forget that the hand holding the key to the hedge has a great scar in its palm, put there for you. He has proved His commitment to you. I may not fully understand every trial in my life, but one thing I know: my Father is using this to conform me to the image of Jesus. I cannot only live with that, but I can even find rest in it.

Job lost everything, including the respect of the community, his friends, and his wife. But he kept maintaining for forty chapters that it was a bum rap, ultimately enticing God to debate him. He felt he deserved better treatment than he was getting. If *he* were God, he would never treat such a good person so poorly.

Finally, Job came to his senses when God straightened out his perspective in chapters 38-41. He saw that he had been trying to justify his performance, and he said in 42:6: "I retract, and I repent in dust and ashes."

When Job acknowledged the sinfulness of his self-justification and turned from it, God said, "Enough!" The goal was accomplished. The flesh's hold on Job was broken. Satan was rebuked (the hedge was repaired), Job was comforted, and his possessions were restored to him doubled. He was even given ten more children to go with the ten he already had in heaven! Job had attained a point of brokenness, never to be the same again.

Peter's experience is another example of this breaking process. He was a "hoss," as we'd call him in Oklahoma. All the guys admired his courage. He was the kid in the fourth grade who was a head taller than the rest of us, remember? He carried the bat outside every recess and took "first bats." Sometimes he'd take four strikes, and we were powerless to stop him.

Through all this success at getting his needs met, Peter developed great self-confidence in his strength. Part of his personal code by which he maintained self-esteem was to never chicken out in a tough spot. Not only could he get his own chestnuts out of any fire, but often those of others as well. He felt he couldn't always trust others, but he could always count on himself. He would never let himself down. He would die first!

"Lord, You can count on me! I'll never let you down," Peter said. "They might try to take You, but it'll be over my dead body!"

"Peter, you're going to deny you even know Me before daylight," Jesus answered. "You're going to turn state's witness to save your hide." And here comes a powerful revelation: "Satan has *obtained by asking permission* to sift you [plural] like wheat; but I have prayed for you [singular], that your [singular] faith may not fail; and you, when once you have turned again, strengthen your brothers" (Luke 22:31, 32, emphasis added; see NASB margin).

This statement was the outgrowth of another of those daily conversations God has with the devil in which He discusses His children and says how proud He is of them. His purpose is to instigate Satan into accusing them. The devil then accuses the believer in his most vulnerable fleshly pattern that correlates with the situation, hoping to prove God wrong. God grants the permission, but He limits Satan to attack *only the flesh from which He wishes to free* the Christian.

I used to put Peter down as a blowhard. But one day I was reading John's account of Jesus' arrest. The text said that Judas "received the Roman cohort" (John 18:3). Not knowing what a cohort was (I didn't even know what a "hort" was), I looked it up. Judas brought six hundred soldiers with him to arrest Jesus! I had always thought it was just a few old men in sheets and a couple of soldiers. The Sunday school quarterly even had a picture of them.

Here they came through the bushes with swords, torches, and armor. I don't know about you, but I'd have counted those odds and headed south! Not Peter. He *did exactly what he bragged he would do*. He pulled his sword, ignored the odds, and waded in, one against six hundred. That dear brother committed suicide for Jesus Christ!

Jesus, however, knowing the plan, told Peter to sheath his sword, then picked up the ear Peter had cut off and put it back on the slave's head. The soldiers led Jesus away, with Peter "following from afar." He was a very confused follower. He was about to get enlightened.

The scene switches to the patio of the high priest. The Matthew 26:69-75 account says that Peter's denial statements were made when he was confronted by women and by unarmed bystanders. Could this be the same man who threw his body at the Roman army? That doesn't make sense. Oh, but it makes glorious sense when we understand what God was up to in Peter's life. He had set out to free Peter from his personal strength.

God and Satan had their daily visit (see Rev. 12:10). I will take the liberty of generalizing from the Job account; that the Father had been telling Satan the disciples were a pretty neat group. "Just look at how well they're coming along," He may have said. "I'm so proud of them. See how loyal they are to me?"

Whereupon the accuser may have said, "Why wouldn't they serve You? You've provided an exciting life for them with future reward. They travel with Your Son performing miracles. They get three square meals a day with lots of prestige. You've got Your hedge around them so nothing bad can happen. But You let me touch that 'darling spot' in their lives, that thing they can't possibly live without, and I'll show You what they're made of. The only reason they're praising You is for what they can get out of it. You let me take Your Son out of the picture and see how long they stay hitched! Let me touch that darling thing in each of them, and they'll bail out on You."

That's exactly the response the Father had set Satan up to make. So, God said, "All right, you may attack their flesh. You may even murder My Son. But you may not kill the eleven." And Satan sifted them when the permission was granted.

Thus, all of a sudden, as Peter was standing in the patio warming his hands, the Evil One supernaturally removed his spine and installed a yellow substitute. Peter's courage evaporated! That thing by which he maintained self-acceptance and pride in himself — to maintain control in each situation — gone. He was proved a coward in the most humiliating way imaginable, by two women and the local "Spit and Whittle Club."

That is the place, however, where all must arrive who would enter into God's rest as spoken of in Hebrews. Peter came to the end of *his* resources, *his* self-justification, *his* self-acceptance, *his* integrity, *his* self-confidence, and *his* rights, all of which had been generated, choreographed, and maintained from years of becoming world-wise at getting his needs met. God was lovingly bringing him to a better kind of security.

After Peter responded properly to this experience of brokenness, God removed the yellow spine, gave him back his own, filled him with the Holy Spirit at Pentecost, and then said to him, "Now, your boldness will be My Spirit through you. It will be loving and gentle, not brazen and self-serving as it was. People are going to see Christ in you, and you will bring great glory and honor to My name" (see Rom. 12:1, 2).

ANSWERS TO QUESTIONS FOR FURTHER STUDY

Chapter 1

1. The Bible says that "God is love." He (God) created you with a need for love so that you would need Him. If you didn't have a need for love, you wouldn't have a need for God.

2. Given the fact that a child learns primarily about himself during the early years, the environment of the home and society can be evaluated to find out what kind of learning took place. The message coming to the child will determine his beliefs about himself and his ability to get his needs met *his* way from the world around him. This will translate into thought, emotion, and behavior (the flesh). By the time the child is able to reason abstractly and see what the circumstances really were, it will be "too late." The habit patterns will already have developed, and the individual will be looking for reinforcement of his feelings, thoughts, and behavior. This will only act to strengthen the fleshly habits.

3. Your answer to this question will be unique to you. The question is designed to help you determine what kind of acceptance methods you have employed independently from God and His provision through Christ. For some, your tools of the trade will be ugly and gross, such as manipulation, profanity, illicit sex, and so on. For others, your acceptance tools will be very socially acceptable. Examples might be service to others, giving gifts, hard work, achievement, and excellent physical condition. Note in regard to the last things mentioned that these characteristics, in and of themselves, are very good. The thing that makes them wrong is

the *motive* for doing them: to gain acceptance independent
of God's provision. The "Flesh Inventory" at the end of this
book (next section) will assist you in discerning your flesh's
traits.

4. The answers to this question and the previous question will
be basically the same. This is not intended to be a trick or a
redundant question. The emphasis is to be placed on
understanding that the methods used to gain acceptance in
the world are the *same methods* used to cut God out of the
picture. If this is grasped, the purpose of the question will
have been successful.

Chapter 2

1. Paul's flesh was primarily developed by Saul, the old, lost
man. Prior to finding Jesus on the Damascus road, he was
independent and rebellious toward God's perfect plan. In order to gain an understanding of *Paul's* flesh and its development, we need to look at *Saul's* lifestyle. The same will hold
true for you. In addition, all saved men can develop fleshly
patterns *after* salvation simply by failing to walk in the
Spirit, trusting the Lord Jesus Christ to meet their needs.

2. Your answer to this question will be similar to questions 3
and 4 in Chapter 1, except that this question is challenging
you to go a step further in terms of understanding. You
should recognize at this time the dynamics of how your flesh
developed, as well as how it manifests itself from time to
time. In addition, we trust you will experience a growing
disdain and dissatisfaction for what you are seeing in your
fleshly motives.

3. Salvation alone! You must be born again. There must have
been the acknowledgement of sin, repentance, and an asking of Jesus to be your Savior and Lord. The ways in
which this takes place in a person's life are as diverse as
God's creative call can be. Trust the Lord to be your guide
as you look at your personal relationship to the Lord Jesus.
And remember, salvation is all that is required to be accepted by God.

Chapter 3

1. Now that you have come to recognize your fleshly patterns, you should be looking for specific ways in which God is choreographing circumstances, challenging you to deal with these areas of fleshly disobedience. He could be doing this in a variety of ways, from something you have read in His Word to a specific circumstance that is causing your flesh stress and pointing you to Christ as the answer.

2. The time that we live here on this earth is the only opportunity we'll have to walk in trust and obedience to the Father. If He automatically erased the learning opportunities that we have (stemming from having to deal with our old, fleshly ways), we would have no chance to grow in the character and likeness of Jesus Christ. We must face these challenges in order to recognize the Lord Jesus' sufficiency in our lives.

3. Although there are many reasons that you could be experiencing frustration at every turn, perhaps the primary point that should be focused on is this: your loving heavenly Father may be trying to break your self-sufficiency, strength, and independence so that you can adequately and willfully cry out to Him as your sufficiency. Unless the Father helps you to realize your insufficiency, you might never recognize His sufficiency. This is often a difficult lesson to learn.

Chapter 4

1. The Bible simply states in Romans 5:12 that all men died in Adam. This means that as a descendant of Adam, you are dead, separated from God, in desperate need of God's salvation through Jesus Christ. There is no solution for this problem other than the execution of the old self and the birth of the new man in Christ. No amount of good works will have an effect as far as earning God's favor on behalf of the old, dead self. This is only rectified through Jesus Christ.

2. Your basic nature is determined by who your spiritual father is. If you are a spirit-descendant of Adam, your basic nature is sinful, rebellious, and independent toward God. If you are a spirit-descendant of the Lord Jesus and a joint heir with Him, you have the laws of God written on your heart. You joyfully concur with the laws of God, and you desire to walk in obedience to the will of the Father.

3. Prior to knowing Jesus Christ as your personal Lord and Savior, you were dead spiritually. With salvation, Jesus Christ literally became your life in the complete fullness of that meaning. He is your purpose. He is your source. He is eternal life. This in no way makes you a hollow tube, a nonentity, or a nonbeing. It simply means that Jesus Christ is wishing to use your personality and earthsuit to manifest His will, character, and nature. On the other hand, you *do not* become a Jesus clone, a little Jesus, or a god. Quite the contrary, you are not Christ, and Christ is not you. Christ is your life, and He wants to live and express His life through your personality, talents, and abilities. A good review of this point is the workshop tools illustration on page 64.

4. It is never a sin for a Christian to be tempted. Jesus "has been tempted in all things as we are, yet without sin" (Heb. 4:15). Therefore, it is very normal for a Christian to be tempted to get his human needs met by rebelling against God's perfect plan. However, it is *not* normal for the Christian to go ahead and sin, as sinning is contrary to the saved person's new nature. The new person looks to Christ to supply all his needs as He promised. Temptation is not a sin until it is accepted by the mind. We aren't saying that the Christian can obtain sinless perfection. As long as we are on this planet, in an earthsuit that is vulnerable to the law of sin, we will be faced constantly with failure to trust Christ's life through us.

Chapter 5

1. Side "B" truths pertain to your being "in" Christ. These principles are imperative to you when you're facing an identity struggle. They will stress to you who you literally are in

Christ, your total acceptance in Him by the Father, and what your situation really is.

2. The thing that died in Christ on the Cross was the old, Adamic life. Some synonyms for this would be the old self, old man, and sin nature.

3. God never intended for *you* to live the Christian life. As a matter of fact, the Christian life is impossible for you to live. There is only one Person who ever lived the Christian life, and that is Jesus Christ. Now, God has placed Christ in you to live and express His life through you. *De*pendence, not *in*dependence, is His plan. Christ through you, not you for Christ.

4. On pages 75-77 you will find a list of Scriptures entitled "My True Identity in Christ." As you review this list of Scriptures as well as track down the many, many more you will find in the Word of God, you should find unique passages that speak to you personally. For example, if you are struggling with feelings of inferiority, perhaps you would find Galatians 3:28 especially meaningful. If you find yourself struggling with guilt, Ephesians 1:7, Romans 3:24, and Romans 8:1 will speak to your being forgiven in Christ.

Chapter 6

1. Satan works through the law of sin, speaking to you with first-person-singular pronouns: I, me, myself, my, and so on. He uses a masculine or feminine "tone of voice" depending upon your sex, and he will accent his statements according to your personal accent. In other words, he impersonates you. Using this technique, he offers up a temptation that correlates with one of your fleshly patterns. Thus, the temptation sounds like you, it seems normal enough to you, and it is something you readily identify with and struggle against. He often tries to get the believer to opt to get a perfectly good human need satisfied via rebellion against God's plan.

2. The original, sinful thoughts the Christian experiences are not generated by the Christian, but by the power of indwell-

ing sin under Satan's control. Sin serves temptation, deception, or accusation up to you, the new creation in Christ,
via the flesh. This communication can come to you during
your quiet time, a prayer time, or during a point of great
vulnerability. You haven't generated this sinful thought. It
has been served up to you by the law of sin. However, the
moment that you choose the thought as yours, you are
covertly sinning in your thought life. Then if you take it for
yourself and act upon it, you have overtly sinned. Only
after choosing to accept the thought do you have sin to confess to the Lord and repent from, not before! The law of sin
cannot *make* you bite on the temptation. You are totally on
the hook to say no to the temptation, and you are likewise
totally on the hook if you say yes.

3. This question is challenging you to take your understanding
   of question 1 from this chapter and personalize that information to your unique version of the flesh. For example, if
   one of your fleshly patterns is for self-condemnation, the law
   of sin might say to you, "I can't believe I'm so stupid. What
   an idiot!" Notice the first-person pronouns that were used.
   Another example might be the person who struggles with
   inferiority: "If I only looked like she looks, I could feel better
   about myself." Once you begin to get the hang of this, you
   will find that you recognize Satan's temptations and accusations much more readily as you trust the Lord Jesus and
   walk in the Spirit. Make sure you use first-person pronouns
   in your answer to this question.

4. The emphasis of your answer to this question should be that
   if you are setting your mind on the fleshly perception you
   have of yourself, you will manifest the ungodly behavior
   that is characteristic of your flesh. On the other hand, if you
   are focusing your attention on your true identity in Christ,
   you will find that you begin to manifest behavior commen-
   surate with who you are in Christ. The Scriptures refer to
   this as the fruit of the Spirit.

5. Your answer should contain something referring to understanding your true identity in Christ and how to cooperate
   with Jesus to let Him live the victorious Christian life

through you. This reflects both sides of the principles we've discussed: Christ in you and you in Christ.

Chapter 7

1. To say that the old man died in Christ is to say that the part of you that was by nature and birth independent and rebellious toward God no longer exists as a result of its execution in Christ at the Cross. You are no longer sinful by nature, separated from God by your heritage, and lost in your trespasses and sins. You are no longer the generator of sinful thoughts; these come from the law of sin. The significance of the death of the old man is evident: you are no longer separated from God by your old, dead spirit, but have been *reborn* as a child of His, a joint heir with Jesus Christ, holy and blameless before Him. You *have become* a new creation in Christ Jesus.

2. On the surface, this question may appear to repeat question 4 in Chapter 5. But this question is challenging you to reiterate to yourself the truths of who you are in Christ. The list of verses given in Chapter 5 pertaining to your true identity in Christ is only a small sample of the vast number of verses that springboard off the verses that are given and illuminate who you really are. The clue to locating these verses will be the word "in" followed by Christ's name or a reference to Him: "in Christ," "in Him," "in whom," and so on. Remember, though, that these verses will do you absolutely no good unless you take them for your own, personal use.

3. "Set your mind on the things above" (Col. 3:2). This is important because God's Word states it imperatively (with great urgency). It is vital in that it is only through setting your mind on things above that you will begin to see the victory of Christ and the characteristics of your true identity manifested in your daily life. Remember how the illustration concerning the rattlesnake demonstrates that the emotions respond to what the mind is set upon. If your mind is set on inadequacy, you will inevitably begin to feel inadequate. If your mind is set on the fact of your acceptance in

Christ, given some time your emotions will begin to respond to this fact. You will never *feel* completely accepted
lest you begin to walk by feel rather than faith. However,
you will begin to experience more points on your emotional
Richter Scale than you previously had. It is imperative that
you set your mind on things above.

4. This exercise will be unique, of course, to the situation you
   have chosen in your life. You should have stressed in your
   answer two primary ideas: first, there should be an emphasis on the side "A" truth of Christ's being your life, living
   and expressing His life through your personality and earthsuit and your cooperating to allow Him to do this. Second,
   there should be some mention of the side "B" truth that you
   are *resting* in the security of your true identity in Christ within the situation. This is what the Word refers to in Hebrews
   as "entering into God's rest." This does not refer to salvation, but to walking in the fullness of the Spirit.

Chapter 8

1. It is of very little importance to consistently *feel* God in your
   life. There will be those times when you do feel the Lord
   and as a result realize He is at work. These periods are very
   enjoyable and reassuring. However, there will probably be
   far more times when there is very little feeling, if any at all,
   that God is anywhere close, let alone dwelling inside you.
   The loving Father has structured the Christian walk in this
   manner in an effort to wean us from walking by feel as op-
   posed to faith, confidence, and dependence on Him. Even if
   your feelings should go in the opposite direction from the
   truth of God's Word, it is imperative that you remain focused
   on what God has said rather than what you may or may not
   feel. Your emotions are not God's barometer of truth; His
   Word is.

2. The man in the cabin was not being hypocritical when he
   began to act as a safe man in the cabin. It was imperative to
   his physical health that he do so. If he had failed to do this,
   he very well could have had a heart attack and died. He was

merely acting on the truth in this situation. It is no different for a Christian who finds himself locked up in the cabin of life with the enemy of God clawing and scratching at the door. Obedience is the key for the Christian who walks according to what God has said in His Word in spite of his fluctuating feelings.

A hypocrite by definition is someone who pretends to be something he is not. Thus, for a Christian who pretends (*acts* like he is) to be fearful, inferior, insecure, *self*-reliant and *self*-confident in spite of God's Word, which speaks to the contrary, hypocrisy would be an apt description. He is acting like something he is not.

Satan's definition of hypocrisy is someone who acts contrary to the way he feels. What a lie! Our feelings may be telling us the direct opposite of what God's truth is. To obey Satan's accusation would be to walk in hypocrisy. To stand our ground against any contrary feelings, looking to the Lord and His Word, is obedience, even though it doesn't feel "right."

3. There are many things that God's Spirit may have shown you as you reflected on Jesus' prayers in the garden. One of the things that stands out in my mind is that Jesus didn't receive lighting-in-sky answers or handwriting on the wall as He prayed to God the Father. Quite the contrary! There was silence from the Father. Not silence showing disapproval, but rather silence indicating trust and comfort. Just because there is no obvious answer to the prayers you pray does not mean that God is ignoring you or is disinterested in you. He has your highest well-being in mind.

Second, Jesus' inability to keep His emotions from soaring should comfort you that the "peace that passes understanding" is not a feeling, but a knowing—knowing that my Father has everything under control in my life as I submit to His will. It's a function of the mind, not the emotions.

Chapter 9

1. The point this question hopes to stress is one of acting on your faith. Perhaps you can more readily see how you effec-

tively walked in faith and obedience or failed to walk by faith and why that failure occurred.

2. There is no way that everything started to go great after Bill began to trust the Lord and walk in the Spirit. Quite the contrary. There were still struggles, difficulties, and trials. Circumstances still closed in from time to time, and Satan continued to offer up his temptations. This reinforces the fact that hardships and trials are merely elements within the laboratory designed to help us learn how to walk in the Spirit. Bill would not have been able to recognize Christ's sufficiency if he hadn't had an opportunity to allow the Lord Jesus to work.

3. The essence of your answer for this question should center on *methodology* rather than results. Are you trusting the Lord Jesus to do the work through you as you do your best or are you doing your best hoping that He will approve of your efforts?

Chapter 10

1. These polarized positions in God's Word leave the devil an opportunity to use even God's Word in an effort to deceive. These "apparent contradictions" are never to be perceived as an evidence that the Bible contains error, but as giving the believer the opportunity to *trust* the Lord God even when faced with apparent "proof" of His inconsistency. This is trusting the integrity of God and "rightly dividing" His Word.

2. The primary key to correctly understanding and interpreting God's Word is to always keep as the central focus Christ on the Cross and what that sacrifice meant to us and for us: God's grace toward us.

3. If you realize that you have made a wrong turn, the proper thing to do is turn around and go back the other direction. The Bible would call this repentance. It is a refocusing of your life on grace and Christ's finished work on the Cross instead of law and performance-based acceptance. This

shouldn't be thought of in terms of backtracking or losing ground. Rather, it is progress in the correct direction toward God's grace. Success in the Christian life is not who finishes the race first, but *how* the race is won.

4. To prevent making a turn toward law, Christ's work on the Cross and God's grace should always be the central focus of your walk. As long as you are focusing on Jesus' atonement for you to interpret God's Word, you will be looking in the proper direction.

Chapter 11

1. There are many reasons that God will use the wilderness in a person's life: to break the Christian from relying on his own strength, to learn trust and obedience, to find rest in Him, and so on. In short, to break the hold the flesh has on his earthwalk.

2. It isn't feasible for a Christian to really know Christ as life and source without going through the wilderness. If you never experience a need, there would never be a reason for Christ to be the supply. God will lovingly *lead* you through the wilderness to intensify that need. The Christian can enter into a commitment with the Lord to know Him as life without having been motivated by stress, but the Father must allow the commitment to be tested if it is to be experiential reality for the believer.

3. Finding yourself in the valley of Achor can practically motivate you to look to the Lord as your sufficiency. Once you have begun to do this, you place yourself in the position of being in God's hands. He is now free to remove you from the valley or to give you the grace to go through it. Either way, you are a winner as you understand God's grace and focus yourself on Him and Him alone as your life.

Chapter 12

1. God allows difficult circumstances in the Christian's life in order to conform him into the image of His Son, Jesus Christ, who lived a life of total dependency on the Father. If

God did not equip the Christian through these actions, He would rob the believer of the opportunity to grow in Christ, experiencing the fullness that knowing Him can bring. It is only through these means that the Christian experientially develops heavenly character traits.

2. Your answer to this question will be unique to you. As you ponder this question, ask the Lord to give you added insight into His unique plan for your life.

3. This question and the next one are asking you to evaluate your personal walk with the Lord. Is He calling you to walk closer, go deeper, trust more? You *must* be maturing. If you aren't, stagnation has set in. Any time you "coast," you are going downhill. Let me encourage you in the Lord. "When God wants to make an oak, He takes a hundred years, but when He wants to make a squash, He takes six months" (Dr. A. H. Strong).

4. See answer 3 above.

FLESH INVENTORY

Ask the Holy Spirit to use this inventory to assist you in identifying what your unique version of the flesh is like. Even though it is true that we are free in Christ, many believers have trouble in identifying what it is they are free from.

Place a number (0-10, where 10 is greater) beside any of these traits with which you *struggle*.

___ Anger
___ Anxiety
___ Argumentative
___ Astrology, Horoscopes, etc. (attracted to)
___ Bigotry
___ Bitterness
___ Boastful
___ Bossy
___ Causing Dissension
___ Conceited
___ Controlled by Emotions
___ Controlled by Peer Pressure
___ Covetousness
___ Critical Tongue
___ Deceitfulness
___ Depression
___ Dominance
___ Drug Dependency
___ Drunkenness
___ Envy (depressed at the good fortune of other's)
___ False Modesty

___ Fear
___ Feelings of Helplessness or Weakness
___ Feelings of Rejection
___ Feelings of Stupidity
___ Feelings of Worthlessness
___ Gluttony
___ Greed
___ Guilt
___ Hatred
___ Hostility
___ Homosexual Lust
___ Idolatry
___ If It Feels Good, Go For It
___ Impatience
___ Impulsiveness
___ Impure Thoughts
___ Inadequate
___ Indifference to Others' Problems
___ Inferiority Feelings
___ Inhibited
___ Insecurity
___ Intemperance

__ Jealousy
__ "Lazyholic"
__ Loner
__ Low Self-Discipline
__ Low Self-Worth
__ Lust for Pleasure
__ Materialistic
__ Must strive to *repay* any kindness shown you
__ Negativism
__ Nervousness
__ Occult (involved in)
__ Opinionated
__ Overly Quiet
__ Overly Sensitive to Criticism
__ Overly Submissive
__ Passivity
__ Prejudice
__ Pride
__ Profane
__ Projecting Blame
__ Prone to Gossip
__ Rebellion at Authority
__ Resentment
__ Restlessness

__ Sadness
__ Self-Centered
__ Self-Confidence
__ Self-Depreciation
__ Self-Gratification (obsessions)
__ Self-Hatred
__ Self-Indulgence
__ Self-Justification
__ Self-Pity
__ Self-Reliant
__ Self-Righteousness
__ Self-Sufficient
__ Selfish Ambition
__ Sensuality
__ Sexual Lust
__ Slow to Forgive
__ Stubbornness
__ Temper
__ Too Quick to Speak
__ Unlovely
__ Vanity
__ Withdrawal
__ Workaholic
__ Worrier

These patterns were generated by the "old man" (or sometimes by the new man walking in carnality) while striving to get your needs met. Though the old man died (Rom. 6:6), the patterns you checked still remain in your brain. These constitute an approximation of your version of the flesh.

Remember now, this inventory is no longer *you* if you are born again. God says, "From now on we recognize no (one) according to the flesh" (2 Cor. 5:16). He recognizes you by your new identity in Christ (see 2 Cor. 5:17).

BIBLIOGRAPHY

Books

Billheimer, Paul. *Don't Waste Your Sorrows*. Christian Literature Crusade, 1977.

Lovett, C. S. *Death: Graduation to Glory*. Personal Christianity, 1974.

Nee, Watchman. *The Normal Christian Life*. Christian Literature Crusade, 1957.

Needham, David. *Birthright*. Multnomah, 1979.

Ortiz, Juan Carlos. *Living with Jesus Today*. Creation House, 1982.

Solomon, Charles. *Handbook to Happiness*. Tyndale House, 1982.

_____. *The Rejection Syndrome*. Tyndale House, 1982.

_____. *Counseling with the Mind of Christ*. Fleming H. Revell, 1977.

Stanford, Miles. *Principles of Spiritual Growth*. Zondervan, 1975.

Taylor, Jack. *The Key to Triumphant Living*. Broadman, 1971.

Trumbull, Charles. *The Life That Wins*. Christian Literature Crusade, 1971.

Pamphlets

Gillham, Anabel. "Faithful Forever." Gillham Ministries, Inc., 1985. (Price: $.75 plus $.60 USPO. This pamphlet tells how to make the truth that you are the Bride of Christ experientially real.)

Gillham, Preston, and Anabel Gillham. "A Study of the Mind." Gillham Ministries, Inc., 1981. (Price: $.50 plus $.60 USPO. This pamphlet tells how to set your mind on things above.)

Audio Tape Albums

Gillham, Bill, and Anabel Gillham. "Victorious Christian Living Seminar." Gillham Ministries, Inc., 1981. (Price: $25.00 plus $1.00 USPO. This package includes a diagram booklet and 8½ hours of teaching on how to apply the truths taught in *Lifetime Guarantee* to your marriage.)

Gillham, Bill, Preston Gillham, and Anabel Gillham. "Advanced Seminar on Victorious Christian Living." Gillham Ministries, Inc., 1985. (Price: $25.00 plus $1.00 USPO. This package includes a diagram booklet and 9 hours of additional teaching on applying the truths taught in *Lifetime Guarantee*. Also includes further emphasis on marriage application.)

Video Seminars

Gillham, Bill, and Anabel Gillham. "Victorious Christian Living." Gillham Ministries, Inc., 1984. (Price: $350.00 plus $5.00 UPS. This package includes eleven video cassettes [50-57 minutes each] dealing with the truths taught in *Lifetime Guarantee* and how to apply them to a marriage. It also includes a 55 page Leader's Discussion Guide. The 40 page viewers Study Guide is available for $1.00 each. Excellent for churches or home cell groups.)

Gillham, Bill, Anabel Gillham, and Preston Gillham. "Advanced Seminar on Victorious Christian Living." Gillham Ministries, Inc., 1986. (Price: $350.00 plus $5.00 UPS. This package includes ten video cassettes [50-53 minutes each] and covers additional teaching on how to apply the truths taught in *Lifetime Guarantee*. Also includes a further emphasis on marriage application.)

Any two video sets may be ordered for $600.00 plus $10.00 UPS.

Free 14 minute promo of the "Victorious Christian Living" Seminar is available upon request.

Inquiries and orders may be sent to:

> Gillham Ministries, Inc.
> 4100 International Plaza, Suite 520
> Fort Worth, Texas 76109
> Phone: (817) 737-6688

If you would like to receive Gillham Ministries' free monthly discipleship paper containing articles on the believer's true identity in Christ along with the Gillham's speaking schedule, please send your printed address to the address given above.

COLOPHON

The typeface for the text of this book is *Baskerville*. Its creator, John Baskerville (1706-1775), broke with tradition to reflect in his type the rounder, yet more sharply cut lettering of eighteenth-century stone inscriptions and copy books. The type foreshadows modern design in such novel characteristics as the increase in contrast between thick and thin strokes and the shifting of stress from the diagonal to the vertical strokes. Realizing that this new style of letter would be most effective if cleanly printed on smooth paper with genuinely black ink, he built his own presses, developed a method of hot-pressing the printed sheet to a smooth, glossy finish, and experimented with special inks. However, Baskerville did not enter into general commercial use in England until 1923.

Substantive editing by Larry Weeden
Copy editing by Michael S. Hyatt
Cover design by Kent Puckett Associates, Atlanta, Georgia
Typography by Thoburn Press, Tyler, Texas
Printed and bound by Maple-Vail Book Publishing Group
Manchester, Pennsylvania
Cover printing by Weber Graphics, Chicago, Illinois